The Legends of
BIRMINGHAM CITY

The Legends of
BIRMINGHAM CITY

by Tony Matthews

breedon **books**
PUBLISHING

First published in Great Britain in 2006 by
The Breedon Books Publishing Company Limited
Breedon House, 3 The Parker Centre,
Derby, DE21 4SZ.

ISBN 1 85983 519 8

Printed and bound by BIDDLES LTD,

King's Lynn, Norfolk.

Contents

Introduction and Acknowledgements

Acknowledgements:

To choose 100 legends from any one club that has been in existence for more than 125 years is no easy task. Therefore, I am expecting a few supporters to ask the question, why wasn't his or her favourite player included?

If I had been allowed to feature 200 legends, I don't think there would be any problems, no queries as to who should and shouldn't be included, but I went for men who I believe gave Birmingham City Football Club excellent service over a number of years.

David Drage, a Blues fanatic and keen statistician, who has been a great friend of mine for many years, asked me to include certain players who he believed warranted an entry, wearing the famous blue and white colours with pride and commitment. I had no objection at all, especially when he mentioned the likes of Colin Green, Bob Hatton, Roger Hynd, Ray Martin, Bert Murray, Garry Pendrey, Paul Peschisolido, Johnny Schofield, Colin Todd, Geoff Vowden, Colin Withers and Ron Wylie.

I would like to thank Dave, Trinity Mirror and Birmingham City Football Club for supplying many of the photographs for this book. Also I say thank you too to Steve Caron, Michelle Grainger and Susan Last at Breedon Books and also love and thanks to my darling wife Margaret for her terrific support and, indeed, patience!

And last but by no means least, I say thank you to the 100 legends themselves, if it hadn't been for them, this book would have been rather nondescript!

Read and enjoy.

Tony Matthews, September 2006

Walter Abbott

Date of birth:	7 December 1877, Small Heath, Birmingham
Died:	1 February 1941, Birmingham

Blues record:

Appearances:	League 77, FA Cup 7, other 1
Goals:	League 57, FA Cup 8, other 1
Debut:	Test Match, 27 April 1896 v Manchester City (h) won 8–0

Also played for: Rosewood Villa, Everton, Burnley, England (1 cap)

For the first five years of his footballing career, from August 1894, Walter Abbott was a strong-running, tenacious inside-left with a cracking shot. On leaving the Blues for Everton in July 1899, he was switched to wing-half from where he produced some sterling performances and scored some splendid goals. He later had a second spell with Blues, from July 1910, but only figured once in the first team and retired with a knee injury in the summer of 1911.

Born within walking distance of Birmingham's former ground, Muntz Street, Abbott played his early football with Rosewood Villa, before joining Blues as a professional in April 1896. He made his Blues debut a couple of days later, in the home Test Match against Manchester City. They were already doomed to relegation, having lost two of their three previous Test Matches and, therefore, had no real pressure on them, but they produced their best form for quite some time, romping to an 8–0 win, Abbott scoring once while assisting in three other goals.

The following season, because of injury, Abbott managed only 12 League outings, scoring four goals, all against Notts County, two at home, two away. Then in 1897–98 he was quite outstanding, bagging 19 goals in 31 games, including his first hat-trick in a 5–1 home win over Darwen. He also struck five braces, but his efforts were in vain as Blues could only finish in sixth place, well off the pace.

After an exceptionally good pre-season, Abbott started 1898–99 like a house on fire, scoring 13 goals in the first 12 matches, six coming in the opening four matches, which included a 6–2 win at Burton. He also created a new individual club scoring record by hitting a five-timer in an 8–0 home League victory over Darwen. He and his left-wing partner Sid Wharton were quite brilliant at times, and, as November gave way to December, Blues looked like promotion material. They maintained their form, as did Abbott, until the turn of the year, but two successive defeats knocked them back, and after that they were always playing catch up – although Abbott was scoring well. Despite his brilliant efforts, which realised a new seasonal club record that still holds good today of 42 goals, 34 in the League, Blues finished a disappointing eighth in the Second Division table, 11 points behind the champions Manchester City. During the second half of that season he netted 16 goals in all games, registering hat-tricks against Loughborough Town (won 6–0), Woolwich Arsenal (won 4–1), Luton Town (won 3–2) and Gainsborough Trinity (won 6–1).

At this juncture, Abbott was enticed away from the club by Everton. He played in the opening three League games of 1899–1900 at inside-left before getting injured. He missed the next two months before returning at left-half, a position he retained with confidence, until 1908 when another injury sent him back into the treatment room. He amassed 291 senior appearances for the Merseysiders, scoring 37 goals. He played in the successive FA Cup Finals of 1906 and 1907, gaining a winners' medal against Newcastle United in the former and a runners'-up medal after defeat by Sheffield Wednesday in the latter. He was also in Everton's 1905 losing semi-final side against eventual runners'-up Aston Villa. Such was his form at Goodison Park that he was capped for England against Wales in March 1902, deputising at centre-half for Frank Forman in a 0–0 draw at Wrexham. He also represented the Football League on four occasions.

Abbott switched his allegiance from Everton to Burnley in July 1908. He spent three useful seasons at Turf Moor, netting 18 goals in 65 senior appearances (the first 13 at left-half, the remainder at inside-left). Blues then re-signed him in readiness for the 1910–11 season, but after just one start – when he lined up at centre-forward on the opening day of the League programme against Fulham at Craven Cottage (lost 3–0) – he was injured and never played again, announcing his retirement from first-class football at the end of the campaign.

Abbott kept in touch with the club and attended several home matches while earning his living working long hours in the car industry at Longbridge. His son, Walter junior, played for Grimsby Town in 1920–21.

Gordon Astall

Date of birth: 22 September 1927, Horwich

Blues record:

Appearances: League 235, FA Cup 27, League Cup 1, Europe 8
Goals: League 60, FA Cup 6, League Cup 1, Europe 0
Debut: League, 17 October 1953 v Bristol Rovers (a) drew 1-1

Also played for: Southampton (amateur), Bolton Wanderers (trial), Plymouth Argyle, Torquay United, England (1 B and 2 full caps)

Regarded by many as the finest outside-right ever to play for Birmingham City, Gordon Astall was a key member of the Blues side that won the Second Division Championship in 1955 and reached the FA Cup Final 12 months later. An amateur with Southampton and a trialist with Bolton Wanderers before signing as a professional for Plymouth in 1947, he had been just as valuable a player when helping Plymouth Argyle win the Third Division South Championship in 1952, the same year he played for England in a B international against France – the first Argyle player for 27 years to gain representative honours. He scored 41 goals in 188 games for the Pilgrims before leaving Home Park for St Andrew's, signed by Blues manager Bob Brocklebank for £14,000 in October 1953 to replace Jackie Stewart.

Astall developed into a regular goalscorer. Blessed with pace and courage, he always tried to get his crosses into the danger-zone quickly, often sending the ball fizzing across the penalty area at no more than shoulder height. Difficult to knock off the ball, he certainly created enough chances for his centre-forwards, Noel Kinsey, Eddie Brown and Peter Murphy, and also for his opposite number on the left flank, Alex Govan, who often ventured into the penalty area to get on the end of Gordon's terrific crosses. Besides laying on chances aplenty for his colleagues, he also scored some superb goals himself, some of them struck home with venom after he had cut in from the wing to set himself up for a shot at goal.

Introduced into the Blues attack a third of the way into the 1953–54 season, Astall netted his first goal for the club in his third outing, a 4–2 win at Derby. He scored twice in 26 outings that season as the Blues finished seventh in the table. The following year he made 37 appearances and netted 11 goals, helping the Blues snatch the title on goal average from Luton Town, with Rotherham United third, Leeds United fourth and Stoke City fifth. In one of the closest promotion battles of all time, there were only two points separating the top-five clubs when the curtain came down on a marvellous season.

Back in the top flight, the Blues did themselves proud, finishing sixth and reaching the FA Cup Final for only the second time in their history. Astall missed only three League games and played in all six Cup ties. He hit 15 goals this time, including 12 in the League, with vital strikes coming in successive 2–2 draws at home to Manchester United and away at Newcastle, right at the start of the campaign, and later in another 2–2 draw at home to Aston Villa and a winner at Tottenham (1–0). He also scored twice in a 3–0 home win over Chelsea when he was outstanding. Unfortunately, he didn't have a great game at Wembley in the Cup Final as the Blues went down 3–1 to Manchester City.

Soon after that Wembley appearance, Astall played twice for England, scoring in both games against Finland and the reigning World champions Germany in 1956. He perhaps deserved more caps than that – but he did have the likes of Stanley Matthews, Tom Finney and Bryan Douglas to contend with! He followed up with an appearance for the Football League against the League of Ireland.

Over the next three seasons Astall played in 120 first-class games for the Blues, helping them reach the semi-finals of the Inter Cities Fairs Cup in 1957 (beaten by Barcelona). However, in 1959–60 his position in the Blues attack came under threat, first from Harry Hooper and then Mike Hellawell, and the following season he was switched to the left wing to get a game. Once Hellawell (on the right) and Brian Taylor (left) established themselves in the side, he moved to pastures new, joining Torquay United in July 1961. He spent two years at Plainmoor and retired from playing in May 1963.

Settling in the Torbay area, Astall coached local side Upton Vale FC for a short time and also worked for an insurance firm. He still enjoys his football today, albeit from his armchair.

Charlie Athersmith

Date of birth: 10 May 1872, Bloxwich, Staffordshire
Died: 18 September 1910, Shifnal, Shropshire

Blues record:
Appearances: League 100, FA Cup 12
Goals: League 6, FA Cup 1
Debut: League, 14 September 1901 v Manchester City (a) won 4–1

Also played for: Bloxwich Wanderers, Bloxwich Strollers (two spells), Unity Gas FC, Aston Villa, Grimsby Town (player for one season, then trainer), England (12 caps)

One of the most famous names in Aston Villa's late 19th-century history, William Charles Athersmith was regarded to be among the fastest wingers of his day. Wonderfully consistent, he was especially adept at racing down the flank for up to 40–50 yards without anyone getting near him and always seemed to rise to the big occasion. One feels that if it hadn't been for West Bromwich Albion's flying winger Billy Bassett, Charlie would have gained many more caps for England than the dozen he was awarded.

A pupil at Walsall Road Council School in Bloxwich, Athersmith developed his football locally and assisted the Birmingham-based Unity Gas works team before joining Villa in February 1891. He spent 10 years with Blues' fiercest rivals and in that time scored 86 goals in 311 first-class appearances. He gained five League Championship-winning medals (1894, 1895, 1897, 1899 and 1900), two FA Cup-winners' medals (1895 and 1897) and was instrumental when Villa completed the coveted League and Cup double in 1897. He was capped 12 times at senior level by England between March 1892 and April 1900 and was on the losing side only twice, scoring three goals, one in a record 13–2 victory over Ireland in February 1899 when he made his international debut on the right wing in Belfast, and in the same forward line that afternoon were his Villa colleagues Dennis Hodgetts on the left flank and Jack Devey at centre-forward. He also appeared in two England international trials (1899 and 1900), played twice for an England XI and represented the Football League on nine occasions, eight against the Scottish League between 1894 and 1901.

In June 1901 Athersmith was snapped up by the Blues, signed to replace the injury-prone Billy Bennett at outside-right. He had an excellent first season, scoring four times in 33 senior games, his first goals for the club coming in a convincing 5–1 home League win over Sheffield United in mid-October. His other three strikes all earned points from 1–1 draws against Stoke, Sunderland and Nottingham Forest. A further six goals were scored the following season in 31 starts, and he was quite superb when Blues hammered hapless Doncaster Rovers 12–0 at home in April as the promotion race from the Second Division gathered momentum. The Blues, in fact, finished runners-up behind Manchester City and Bolton Wanderers, while Charlie's future employers Grimsby Town dropped out of the top flight.

At this juncture, Athersmith was not getting any younger, but he still produced the goods at the highest level, missing only one League game (away to Notts County on Boxing Day) as the Blues established themselves in the First Division by claiming 11th place in the table. He remained at the club for one more season (1904–05), which saw him make his 100th and final League appearance for the Blues in a 0–0 draw at Meadow Lane against Notts County. He was replaced on the right wing by Charlie Tickle.

Unwilling to retire, the 33-year-old player was then selected for an unsanctioned Tagg and Campbell FA tour to Germany in the summer of 1905. He regretted going in the end because he, and several other players, many of them internationals, were subsequently suspended, and, in effect, his career at top level ended there and then. He later played briefly for one of his former clubs Bloxwich Strollers during the 1906–07 season while still serving out his ban, and when that was lifted he became senior trainer at Grimsby Town, offering to play if required, but he never made the first team. He held his position as spongeman until May 1909 when he became ill and moved to Shifnal. He was only 38 when he died.

Bertie Auld

Date of birth: 23 March 1938, Maryhill, Glasgow

Blues record:
Appearances: League 125, FA Cup 6, League Cup 10, Europe 4
Goals: League 26, FA Cup 0, League Cup 4, Europe 1
Debut: Inter Cities Fairs Cup, 3 May 1961 v Inter Milan (h) won 2–1

Also played for: Panmure Thistle, Maryhill Harp, Celtic (two spells), Dumbarton, Hibernian (also coach), Scotland (3 caps)
Managed: Partick Thistle (two spells), Hibernian, Hamilton Academical, Dumbarton

Celtic chairman Robert Kelly wasn't happy with Bertie Auld's attitude during the late 1950s, and as a result he asked manager Jimmy McGrory to transfer him, which he did, to Birmingham City for £15,000. Originally a full-back, he was converted into a left-winger at the age of 16 before joining Celtic as a professional in March 1955. He had netted 24 goals in 86 first-class appearances, gained three full caps for his country and played twice for the Scottish League before leaving Parkhead in April 1961 – just in time to play in the second leg of that season's Inter Cities Fairs Cup semi-final against Inter Milan, helping the Blues win 4–2 on aggregate to qualify for the Final versus another Italian club, AS Roma.

Possessing good skills, Auld became a huge favourite with the Blues supporters, although his fiery temper continued to annoy referees and his manager! He took over the left-wing berth from Brian Taylor and had a fine first full season at St Andrew's, netting six times in 43 outings, his first strike proving to be the winner in a 2–1 home League victory over Bolton in September 1961. Later in the month he lined up in the first leg of the Fairs Cup Final, which finished 2–2, and soon afterwards was cautioned (with others) in a fiery return leg in Rome as the Blues lost 2–0 (4–2 on aggregate).

A player who hated being pushed around, he retaliated far too often, and during his career (in Scotland and England) he was sent off five times, taking an early bath as a Blues player against RCD Español in a Fairs Cup game in December 1961, after a scuffle with the Spanish defender Vidour Rivas.

During 1962–63 Auld was outstanding, despite the Blues struggling in the League. Indeed, they only just managed to escape relegation, finishing 20th in the table, two points above Manchester City, thanks to a last match 3–2 win over Leicester. However, it was a completely different story in the League Cup as Blues surged through to the Final, Auld claiming four goals, including vital ones against Notts County in round four and Bury in the first leg of the semi-final, both matches ending in 3–2 victories. City neighbours Aston Villa were Blues' opponents in the two-leg Final, and he produced the goods in the home clash at St Andrew's, which ended in a 3–1 win. He was kept quiet at Villa Park, but the Blues defence held firm to earn a 0–0 draw and so lifted their first ever major trophy.

Retaining his position on the left flank, Auld, who had Welshman Ken Leek as his partner, scored 10 goals in 1963–64 – his best return for the Blues. Five came in November, including a brace in a 3–3 draw with Nottingham Forest and also a fine winning effort at Chelsea. Blues, though, had to battle hard and long once again to escape the drop, a last match win over Sheffield United securing their top-flight status. It was much of the same the following season as they again struggled on the field, despite some more enterprising displays from Bertie. It was a surprise to a lot of fans when, in January 1965, Celtic boss Jock Stein swooped to take him back to Scotland for £12,000.

Back at his old hunting ground Auld became a key member of the Celtic team, and with Tommy Gemmill behind him and Bobby Murdoch alongside they formed a terrific left-sided trio. He helped the Bhoys win five Scottish League titles in succession (1966–70), three Scottish Cup Finals (1965, when he scored twice against Dunfermline, 1967 and 1969), the League Cup four times in a row (1967 to 1970) and the coveted European Cup in 1967 as well as playing in the World Club Championship.

In May 1971 – after taking his goal tally to 79 in 277 first-class appearances – Auld joined Hibernian, later becoming coach at Easter Road. Thereafter, he enjoyed managerial spells at Partick Thistle (1974–80 and 1986–88), Hibs (1980–81), Hamilton Academical (1982–83) and Dumbarton (1988–89).

Bertie – who was christened Robert – now resides in Glasgow.

Jack Badham

Date of birth: 31 January 1919, Birmingham
Died: 1 January 1992, Birmingham

Blues record:
Appearances: League 175, FA Cup 13, Europe 2
Goals: League 4, FA Cup 0, Europe 0
Debut: League, 26 February 1948 v Chesterfield (a) won 3–0

Also played for: Shirley Juniors, Stourbridge, Moorlands Athletic
Managed: Moor Green

Versatile defender Jack Badham was associated with the Blues for 23 years. Birmingham-born, he joined the club as an amateur in the summer of 1934, turned professional in May 1946 and left for Stourbridge in May 1957. Unfortunately he lost six years of his footballing career during World War Two when he served in the Army, hardly ever getting a game, certainly not with the Blues.

After the hostilities, Badham twice helped Birmingham gain promotion from the Second Division, firstly in the 1947–48 season, although he managed only two appearances, and secondly in 1954–55, when he played in 11 League games. Having made his Blues debut in February 1948, when he replaced Fred Harris at Chesterfield in a Second Division game, he scored his first goal for the club at senior level in a surprise 3–0 home League win over champions-elect Portsmouth in April 1949 but was surprisingly only a first-team regular with the Blues for three seasons: 1949–50, 1950–51 and 1951–52. In fact, he made 110 of his 190 first-class appearances during that time, the majority coming at right-back while Ken Green or Dennis Jennings played alongside him on the left. He also appeared at centre-forward in one game, replacing the injured Jim Dailey in a 1–0 defeat at Middlesbrough in October 1949. 'I didn't like it one bit' he said afterwards. Sadly, having made 17 appearances during the 1955–56 season, he missed the FA Cup Final when manager Arthur Turner selected Johnny Newman ahead of him to take over at left-half in place of the injured Roy Warhurst. However, he did appear in the FA Cup semi-finals of 1951 and 1956, and he also lined up in the Blues' first ever European game against Inter Milan in the Inter Cities Fairs Cup in May 1956, playing his part in a 0–0 draw at the San Siro.

A huge favourite with the home supporters, Badham was a lion-hearted footballer who occupied eight different positions during his time at St Andrew's. Preferring one of the two full-back berths, it was at right-back where he finally established himself in the first team during the 1949–50 campaign – 15 years after first joining the club from the local intermediate team, Shirley Juniors.

As time progressed and Badham got older, England international Jeff Hall and Ken Green became the chosen full-back pairing, and in fact, they were regulars in the side (when fit and available) from January 1953 onwards (until Jack left in 1957). During that four-and-a-half year period he was used either as a right-half or centre-half, and when he was called into action he never once let the side down. Known around St Andrew's as 'Mr Reliable', he never asked for a transfer and, above all, was never dejected when he was left out of the starting line up in favour of another player, or when he was confined to playing in the reserves. Indeed, he skippered the Blues second XI for two seasons, enjoying every minute of the action in the London Combination when he brushed shoulders with some pretty useful footballers, some of them former and future internationals.

Badham loved playing for Birmingham City, and in truth he would have liked to have stayed longer than he did at St Andrew's. He eventually departed at the age of 38, released by his boss Arthur Turner, who stated publicly that he 'Had been a loyal and dedicated servant to Birmingham City Football Club.' On leaving the club in the summer of 1957, he signed for Birmingham League side Stourbridge before returning to St Andrew's to work as a coach, later serving Moorlands Athletic as a player-coach and also managing Moor Green.

A very useful golfer, Jack lived in Birmingham all his life and was 72 when he died.

Ned Barkas

Date of birth:	21 November 1901, Wardley, Northumberland
Died:	24 April 1962, Little Bromwich, Warwickshire

Blues record:

Appearances:	League 260, FA Cup 28
Goals:	League 9, FA Cup 0
Debut:	League, 29 December 1928 v Manchester City (a) won 3–2

Also played for: St Hilda's Old Boys, East Borden, Hebburn Colliery, Bedlington United (two spells), South Shields, Wardley Colliery, Norwich City (amateur), Huddersfield Town, Chelsea, Solihull Town (player-manager), Willmott Breedon FC, Nuffield Mechanics

Edward Barkas started his footballing career as a centre-forward and once scored five goals in a Cup game for Bedlington United. After spending several years playing in non-League football and being employed as a collier, he joined Huddersfield Town as a professional in January 1921 and was immediately converted into a defender, eventually developing into a tough-tackling, hard-working, strong-kicking full-back, never showy or spectacular, just reliable and consistent, authoritative and influential.

Establishing himself in the first XI during the 1921–22 season, Barkas went on to make 131 senior appearances for the Terriers, gaining successive League Championship-winning medals in 1922–23 and 1923–24, but he missed out on a third having being ousted out by Roy Goodall. He also appeared in the 1928 FA Cup Final when Huddersfield were defeated by Blackburn Rovers and in the summer of 1926 toured Canada with the FA party. In December 1928 he was recruited by Birmingham manager Leslie Knighton for a then club-record fee of £4,000, and what a terrific signing he tuned out to be.

Barkas went straight into the team at right-back as partner to Jack Randle, and over the next eight-and-a-half years, during which time he switched over to the left flank, he appeared in 288 senior games and skippered Blues in the 1931 FA Cup Final against Midlands neighbours West Bromwich Albion, for whom his old Leeds Road colleague George Shaw played at full-back. Unfortunately, despite keeping Baggies' winger and captain Tommy Glidden quiet, he was only able to collect another runners'-up medal as Blues went down 2–1 on a soggy, strength-sapping Wembley pitch.

From his Blues debut against Manchester City in December 1928 until his departure in April 1937, Barkas produced many outstanding performances. He was never given a roasting by an opposing winger, and if it hadn't been for the form shown by Ernie Blenkinsopp of Sheffield Wednesday and also Eddie Hapgood of Arsenal he may well have gained a full England cap. He came close, but not close enough, sitting on the bench as a reserve for two home internationals.

Blues manager Knighton left St Andrew's to take over as boss of Chelsea in 1933, and four years later he decided to sign a then 36-year-old Barkas on a free transfer to bolster up, and indeed add some experience and quality to, his defence. Although lacking in pace, he played regularly for the London club during the 1937–38 campaign, before age and fitness caught up with him. He remained at Stamford Bridge until May 1939 when he chose to quit top-class football. He immediately returned to the Midlands to take over as player-manager of Solihull Town and later assisted Willmott Breedon FC (1943–44) and Nuffield Mechanics (1944–45) while working as a charge-hand on munitions during World War Two.

Barkas was the eldest of five bothers, four of whom played football at professional level, and they collectively appeared in 1,125 League games between 1920 and 1949. Ned made 404 appearances, Sam, who starred for Bradford City, Manchester City and England, totalled 377, Tom, who also served with Bradford City, played in 279 and Harry, ex-Gateshead and Liverpool, accumulated 45. The fifth brother, James, was briefly with West Bromwich Albion but failed to make the first team. He was also the cousin of Walter Felton, who starred for Manchester City, Sheffield Wednesday, Tottenham Hotspur and England, while his uncle, Tom Godfrey, played for Blackpool.

Percy Barton

Date of birth: 19 August 1895, Plaistow, London
Died: 12 October 1961, London

Blues record:
Appearances: League 331, FA Cup 18
Goals: League 13, FA Cup 1
Debut: League, 3 January 1914 v Notts County (h) won 2–1

Also played for: Tottenham Thursday FC, Tottenham Hotspur (guest), Edmonton Amateurs, Sultan FC, Stourbridge, England (7 caps)

Percy Barton, a former butcher's errand boy, was a thick-set wing-half, able to occupy both flanks who, towards the end of his career, appeared in the left-back position. A dour, industrious defender, clever at breaking up attacks and plying his forwards with seductive passes, he often fell foul of referees with his over-robust play, and during his career he was sent off on four occasions, three while playing for the Blues.

Barton joined Blues as a full-time professional on New Year's Day in 1914 and made his senior debut three days later in the home League game against Notts County, when, taking over from Joe Smith, he became the fifth player to be used in the problematic left-half position that season. He made 19 appearances in that penultimate pre-war campaign and followed up with another 42 (in League and FA Cup) in 1914–15, helping Blues finish a creditable sixth in the Second Division.

Unfortunately, World War One severely interrupted Barton's career as a Blues player, as it did many other footballers, and, in fact, during the hostilities he made only nine first-team appearances for the club, while making almost 90 as a guest player for Spurs, the team he supported as a lad. He was a regular in the Spurs side for two seasons (1915–17), helping them clinch the runners'-up prize in the London Combination Second Competition in 1916. He also had a few outings in the inside-left position for the Londoners.

When peacetime League football resumed in August 1919, Barton slotted into the half-back line along with Jack Roulson and Alex McClure and missed only one game out of a possible 45 in the League and FA Cup as Blues finished third in Division Two, missing promotion by eight points. The following season he missed only one League game (at home to Nottingham Forest in April) as Blues won promotion, just pipping Cardiff City on goal average to clinch the Second Division title on the last day of the campaign after a 2–0 win at Port Vale. He was in fine form around this time and his efforts were rewarded when he won the first of seven full caps for England, lining up against Belgium in Brussels in May 1921 (won 2–0). He played against Ireland in Belfast five months later and appeared in his last five internationals between October 1923 and October 1924, starring for England in the first game against Scotland at Wembley.

Barton comfortably held his place in the Blues side until 1927, although at times niggling knee and ankle injuries and the odd suspension kept him on the sidelines. He went on to accumulate 349 competitive appearances for Blues, scoring 14 goals, one of them a stunning header from fully 30 yards during a 4–1 home League victory over Wolves in November 1920. His first goal for the club came in a 6–3 home win over Leeds City in October 1914 and his last was scored against Sunderland at St Andrew's in January 1925, exactly nine years after his Blues debut.

On leaving Blues in August 1929, Barton joined local non-League side Stourbridge. He continued playing for another four years, finally hanging up his boots in May 1933, shortly before his 38th birthday. He continued to attend Birmingham's home matches at St Andrew's before returning to his birth city of London where he died in 1961 at the age of 66.

Malcolm Beard

Date of birth: 3 May 1942, Cannock, Staffordshire

Blues record:
Appearances: League 350+1, FA Cup 24+1, League Cup 25, Europe 4
Goals: League 26, FA Cup 4, League Cup 2, Europe 0
Debut: League, 17 September 1960 v Burnley (a) lost 2–1

Also played for: Aston Villa, Atherstone Town, England (4 Youth caps)

Malcolm Beard served Birmingham City Football Club for 16 years, 14 of them as a player. He represented both Cannock & District and Staffordshire Schools and joined the club as a 15-year-old straight from St Chad's School, Cannock, in June 1957, turning professional in May 1959.

Able to play as an inside-forward or wing-half, Beard developed fast, and made his name in second-team football before being handed his senior Blues debut by manager Gil Merrick in September 1960 against the reigning League champions Burnley in front of almost 21,000 fans at Turf Moor, taking over from the injured Dick Neal at left-half. He played in the next two League games of that season and also in a third-round League Cup replay at Plymouth. Then in 1961–62 he bedded himself permanently in the Blues side, being an ever present and scoring his first goal in the last game of the campaign in a 3–2 defeat at Tottenham.

In 1962–63 Beard suffered a few injury problems, but when fit he once again proved what a fine performer he was, helping Blues win the League Cup and also escape relegation to the Second Division, this after a frantic last month when seven points were gained, including a nail-biting last gasp win over the FA Cup finalists Leicester City at St Andrew's. He was outstanding in the two-leg League Cup Final against Aston Villa. He drove forward at every opportunity during the home encounter and was resolute in defence in the return fixture at Villa Park as the Blues preserved their 3–1 lead to lift the trophy – the club's first in a major competition.

Beard was absent from only six League games in 1963–64, when Blues yet again escaped the drop by the skin of their teeth. However, his efforts the following season proved worthless as Blues went down, finishing bottom of the First Division, but he did have the pleasure of scoring a hat-trick in an exciting 5–5 home draw with Blackburn Rovers in the penultimate League fixture – sadly only 8,877 hardy supporters bothered to turn up to see it.

It was a disappointing time for the club, but Beard stuck in there and, with the rest of the players, vowed to make a bold effort to regain top-flight status. The next two League games were pretty mediocre, although he did return his best goal haul in 1965–66 with a total of 10, and he also helped his side reach the semi-final of the League Cup in 1967, beaten by the eventual winners Queen's Park Rangers. And then, in 1967–68, Malcolm and Blues again fell at the crucial hurdle, losing to Midlands neighbours West Bromwich Albion 2–0 in the semi-final of the FA Cup.

Unfortunately, the next two seasons of League football were not much better, Blues claiming seventh and 18th places in the Second Division respectively, but Beard always gave his best. He went on to reach two personal milestones in 1970–71: 350 League appearances and 400 senior appearances for the club. He was unlucky to get sent off in his last ever game for Blues, against Millwall in December 1970.

In July 1971 Beard made the brave decision to leave St Andrew's for Aston Villa, where he spent two seasons and appeared in four games when Villa won the Third Division title in 1972. He ventured into non-League football with Atherstone Town, coached in Saudi Arabia from 1974 and returned to St Andrew's as senior scout in 1979, later taking a similar position at Villa Park (1982–86) before working as a coach at Middlesbrough and Portsmouth. He served Leicester City in a scouting capacity in 1990 and returned to Villa for a third time in 1994 as chief scout, taking over the second team in 1997. Malcolm was in football for over 40 years.

Terry Hennessey once said 'If you had 11 men in your team like Malcolm, you couldn't go wrong.'

Jimmy Bloomfield

Date of birth:	15 February 1934, Kensington, London
Died:	3 April 1983, Chingford, Essex

Blues record:

Appearances:	League 123, FA Cup 8, League Cup 10, Europe 7
Goals:	League 28, FA Cup 0, League Cup 2, Europe 2
Debut:	League Cup, 14 November 1960 v Plymouth Argyle (h) drew 0–0
Also played for:	Hayes, Brentford (two spells), Arsenal, West Ham United, Plymouth Argyle, Leyton Orient (player-manager), England (2 Under-23 caps)
Managed:	Leicester City, Leyton Orient (second spell)

Jimmy Bloomfield represented the Middlesex County Youth team as a teenager and assisted Hayes of the Athenian League for a little over two seasons before joining Brentford as a professional in October 1952. A skilful, ball-playing inside-forward, he made over 40 League appearances in his first spell with the Bees, and then, following his £10,000 transfer from Griffin Park to Highbury in July 1954, he proceeded to give Arsenal excellent service for well over six years, during which time he accumulated a very fine record of 236 senior appearances, scoring 60 goals, and gained two England Under-23 caps in 1956–57, played for the Football League against the Scottish League in March 1960 and represented London in the Fairs Cup Final. He also completed his national service in the Army and played in several representative games for them.

On losing his place in the Gunners' side to George Eastham, Bloomfield switched from north London to Birmingham City in October 1960, Blues boss Gil Merrick paying £30,000 for his signature and saying at the time 'This player is one of the best in his position in the First Division.' He had a quiet debut for Blues in a 0–0 League Cup draw at Plymouth, but things were made worse five days later when his first League game for the club ended in a crushing 6–0 defeat at the hands of double-chasing Tottenham Hotspur at White Hart Lane. Thankfully, that disastrous result – Blues heaviest defeat away from home for five years – was soon forgotten, and, linking up with Brian Taylor on the left wing, Jimmy started to produce the goods expected of him – although Blues still struggled in the League, losing three of their next four matches.

The introduction of centre-forward Jimmy Harris into the attack saw things look up on the pitch and before the turn of the year Blues were showing signs of improvement. And Bloomfield, besides creating chances for his colleagues, found time to score his first goal for the club in a vital 2–1 home win over Newcastle United on Boxing Day.

In January 1961, having earlier appeared in the second leg of the Inter Cities Fairs Cup Final against AS Roma, Bloomfield was switched to the inside-right berth, and from then until the end of the season he alternated between that and inside-left as Blues kept clear of relegation despite losing their last five League matches. In 1961–62 he missed seven League games and scored 11 goals, following up in 1962–63 with 11 more, including two in the League Cup, which Blues won, beating Aston Villa 3–1 in the two-leg Final. With Mike Hellawell now on the wing, they formed a pretty useful partnership that lasted until April 1964 when Jimmy returned to his former club Brentford. He had done well with Blues, averaging a goal every five games.

In October 1965 Bloomfield moved to south Devon, signing for Plymouth Argyle, and in March 1968 he became player-manager of Leyton Orient, retiring as a player in May 1969 with over 550 senior appearances under his belt (495 in the Football League). He was in charge of Leicester City from June 1971 to May 1977 before having a second spell in the hot seat at Orient, from September 1977 to August 1981. In his first spell at Brisbane Road, he guided Orient to the Third Division Championship in 1970, and in 1978, after his return, he took the London club into the semi-finals of the FA Cup. As boss of Leicester, he lost the 1971 FA Cup semi-final in a replay and won the FA Charity Shield. Ill-health forced him to retire as Foxes manager, and he took a part-time position as scout with Luton Town, where he was at the time of his tragic death in April 1983.

Len Boyd

Date of birth: 11 November 1923, Plaistow, London

Blues record:
Appearances: League 256, FA Cup 25, Europe 1
Goals: League 13, FA Cup 1, Europe 0
Debut: League, 22 January 1949 v Preston North End (a) drew 0–0

Also played for: Ilford, Plymouth Argyle, Hinckley Athletic, England B (1 cap)

Right-half Len Boyd skippered Birmingham City to the Second Division Championship in 1954–55 and then led them in the FA Cup Final against Manchester City at Wembley the following season.

After attending and playing for the same West Ham School as another Blues player, Ken Green, Boyd started his footballing career in earnest with non-League side Ilford. He served in Malta with the Royal Navy during World War Two before spending four years as a professional with Plymouth Argyle, for whom he scored five goals in 80 senior appearances.

Transferred to St Andrew's for £17,500 in January 1949, signed by manager Bob Brocklebank, Boyd was the first player to leave the Devon club for a five-figure fee, and Blues certainly benefitted from his experience at a lower level. He went straight into the first team, joining Fred Harris and Ted Duckhouse in the half-back line for the First Division encounter with Preston North End at Deepdale, and the following season he established himself as a regular member of the team, making 27 appearances as Blues, unfortunately, were relegated from the top flight.

Boyd and Blues were to spend the next five seasons in Division Two, twice coming close to winning promotion, in 1951 and 1952, and also reaching the semi-finals of the FA Cup when they were beaten in a replay by Blackpool in March 1951. Taking over as team captain, he proved to be an inspirational leader, and he was outstanding when Blues regained their top-flight status in 1955, going up as champions. A year later he played in the FA Cup Final and also tasted European football for the first time via the Inter Cities Fairs Cup competition, making his Blues debut in this competition against the Yugoslavian side Dinamo Zagreb. Blues reached the semi-final stage of that tournament but lost a three-pronged confrontation with the Spanish giants Barcelona, by which time Len had left the club.

Capped by England B against Holland B in 1951–52, his only representative honour, Boyd was a fine player and a hard-working footballer who was successfully converted into a wing-half after starting out as a useful inside-forward while serving in the Royal Navy. He certainly gave Blues great service, appearing in 282 first-class matches and figuring prominently with two England internationals on the right – Jeff Hall behind him and Gordon Astall in front of him. Astall, in fact, was also a teammate of his at Plymouth.

In the summer of 1956 Boyd announced his retirement from first-class football at the age of 32, calling it a day because of a niggling knee injury that had affected his game over the previous six months. Indeed, injections had kept him going most of the time. He was out of football for well over two years before making a mini comeback with non-League side Hinckley Athletic in January 1959. Unfortunately, he couldn't manage a full game and at that point he knew his time was up. He remained in the game, being employed as coach and chief scout by Redditch United, before settling down in Melton Mowbray, Leicestershire.

Joe Bradford

Date of birth:	22 January 1901, Peggs Green, Leicestershire
Died:	6 September 1980, Birmingham

Blues record:

Appearances:	League 414, FA Cup 31
Goals:	League 249, FA Cup 18
Debut:	League, 25 December 1920 v West Ham United (a) drew 1–1

Also played for: Coleorton, Peggs Green Victoria, Bristol City, England (12 full caps)

A very sporting player, Joe Bradford – who was born on the day Queen Victoria died – revealed marksmanship and shooting power of the highest calibre, and his haul of 267 first-class goals for Blues remains to this day a club record, probably never to be beaten.

Surprisingly, Bradford had the opportunity to join Aston Villa. He had been scoring regularly in Leicestershire junior football, bagging 14 goals for Peggs Green Victoria against Birstall Rovers in April 1919, having earlier notched 65 in the 1915–16 season for Coleorton, when Villa invited him along for a trial. He turned up but was rather timid and nervous, and when no one within the club offered to pay his expenses he refused to come back for a second time. He also had an unsuccessful trial with Derby County before Blues stepped in and asked him along to St Andrew's – and offered to pay his expenses!

Bradford did well and was immediately taken on as a professional, signing the appropriate forms on 11 February 1920, Blues handing his former club Coleorton a cheque for £125. Initially groomed in the reserves, and acting as cover for Harry Hampton and Joe Lane, he was given an occasional run out in the first team as Blues headed towards the Second Division Championship in 1920–21. Then, once Birmingham were in the top flight, his opportunities increased – and he quickly made his mark with some superb displays. He scored 10 goals in 17 League games, including two fine efforts in a 2–1 win at Bolton and two more in a 4–3 home victory over Middlesbrough.

Strong and mobile with a fair amount of skill, Bradford struck 19 goals in 1922–23 and claimed 24 the following season – 20 more than Blues' second top scorer! He also gained the first two of his 12 full international caps for England, lining up and scoring against Ireland on his debut and then notching up a brace in a 4–0 win over Belgium two months later. It would be five years before he won his third cap, but in between times he represented the Football League on five occasions.

During the second half of 1924–25, Bradford was injured and as a result hit only 11 goals, but he was back to his best 12 months later when he netted 27 times in total, including hat-tricks against Tottenham Hotspur (home) and Blackburn Rovers (away). Over the next five seasons (1926–31) he weighed in with 129 goals, 32 coming in 1927–28, his best seasonal tally. In September 1929 he scored 11 goals in the space of eight days: three for Blues against Newcastle United, five for the Football League versus the Irish League and another three for Blues against Blackburn Rovers. He also netted in the 1931 FA Cup Final against West Bromwich Albion – but the game ended in defeat and this was a bitter disappointment for him.

In his last four seasons at St Andrew's Bradford scored 51 goals before injuries caught up with him, and he was transferred to Bristol City in May 1935. He retired a year later to become a café owner in Birmingham and then managed pubs in Stourbridge, Droitwich and Birmingham as well as helping the former Aston Villa player Eric Houghton run a sports shop. He also served as president of Sutton Town FC, scouted for Arsenal (1946–47) and worked in the pools office at St Andrew's in the late 1960s.

Bradford's brother William played for Walsall, while his cousin, Hugh Adcock, served with Corinthians, Leicester City and Bristol Rovers and won five England caps, three with Joe in 1929 versus France, Spain and Ireland.

Kevan Broadhurst

Date of birth: 3 June 1959, Dewsbury, Yorkshire

Blues record:
Appearances: League 147+6, FA Cup 13, League Cup 7
Goals: League 10, FA Cup 0, League Cup 0
Debut: League, 12 February 1977 v Norwich City (h) won 3–2

Also played for: Walsall, Knowle North Star, Sherwood Celtic (two spells)
Managed: Birmingham City (caretaker/joint), Knowle North Star, Northampton Town, Walsall

Kevan Broadhurst was a gritty Yorkshireman and a hard-tackling player who could perform in several positions, preferring a central-midfield slot, although for half a season, following the departure of Joe Gallagher in 1981, he took over at centre-half. Excellent in the air for a short man, he never lacked fighting spirit and was a never-say-die competitor whose career, unfortunately, was dogged by a catalogue of niggling ankle and knee injuries.

Broadhurst had unsuccessful trials with Bradford City and Manchester City before Blues scout Don Dorman stole him from under the noses of Leeds United and sent him along to St Andrew's. He joined the club as an apprentice in July 1975 and turned professional in March 1977 after some excellent displays in the youth and reserve teams. He scored on his senior Blues debut in mid-February 1977 against Norwich City (won 3–2) but was injured in his second game against West Bromwich Albion a fortnight later. It was not until the following September that he got back into the first team, and although still classed as a reserve he made 10 appearances that term, following up with another 18 in 1978–79 when, sadly, Blues were relegated to the Second Division.

In February 1979 Broadhurst was selected to play for the England Under-21 side against Holland in Alkmaar, only for the match to be called off due to an icy pitch. He never got another chance to represent his country.

Biding his time for a while after that, Broadhurst had a loan spell with Walsall (three games) before being called upon to take over at right-back by manager Jim Smith in December 1979. He did very well, playing his part in helping Birmingham regain top-flight status that season by finishing in third place.

Injuries meant that Broadhurst made only 15 appearances in 1980–81, but the following term he had his best spell in the first XI, starring in 38 competitive games, over half of them at centre-half. He continued at the heart of the Blues defence the following season and again in 1983–84 (when relegation was suffered yet again) before injuries began to take their toll. He struggled desperately at times in the treatment room, but in the end his brave efforts proved fruitless, and he was forced to retire in March 1986 at the age of 26, although he did try his luck briefly with a local, non-League outfit Knowle North Star, becoming the club's general manager in 1991–92. He later had a few games with Sherwood Celtic (January–March 1992) and was appointed caretaker manager of Knowle in August 1993, returning to St Andrew's the very next month to become Blues' youth-team coach, later acting as caretaker and then joint manager, before reverting back to youth-team duties when Barry Fry took charge of the first team. He combined his duties by again assisting Sherwood Celtic, and in October 2001 he re-entered League football as manager of Northampton Town, later taking over the hot seat from Paul Merson at relegation-threatened Walsall.

Eddie Brown

Date of birth: 28 February 1926, Preston

Blues record:

Appearances: League 158, FA Cup 18, Europe 9
Goals: League 74, FA Cup 13, Europe 3
Debut: League, 16 October 1954 v Swansea Town (h) won 2–0

Also played for: Preston North End, Southampton, Coventry City, Leyton Orient, Scarborough, Stourbridge, Bedworth Town, Wigan Athletic
Managed: Bedworth Town

As a youngster, Eddie Brown wanted to join the church but was persuaded not to by a football-mad clergyman. He certainly made the right decision – as he became a more than useful, if somewhat unorthodox, centre-forward who had a very interesting professional career that spanned 16 years.

After deciding against joining the cloth, Brown signed for Preston North End in 1948, and after spending a few years with both Southampton and Coventry City he joined Birmingham City in October 1954. He became an instant success at St Andrew's after taking over the number-nine jersey, vacated by Cyril Trigg the season before. He went on to average a goal every two games for Blues, and his haul of 14 in 1954–55 helped Arthur Turner's side win the Second Division Championship. The following season he was again in tip-top form, netting another 28 goals, including seven in the FA Cup, as Blues went through to the Final, but they lost to Manchester City. And in 1956–57, when Blues again reached the FA Cup semi-finals, he weighed in with a further 19 goals, just nine behind leading marksman Alex Govan.

Occasionally, after scoring a goal, spectacular or not, Brown would peel away and do a celebratory jig around one of the corner flags, but he was like that; he simply loved scoring goals and he certainly enjoyed his football – a great character on and off the pitch.

Brown's first goal for Blues came in his second outing and it earned a point from a 1–1 draw with Derby County. Six weeks later he was on fire when scoring a hat-trick as Blues thrashed Liverpool 9–1 at St Andrew's, and later in the season he netted two beauties in a 5–2 win at Middlesbrough and set the ball rolling with a goal in the vital promotion-seeking encounter at Doncaster on the last day of the League campaign when Blues won 5–1 to beat Luton Town on goal average and clinch the Second Division title.

Another treble the following season, in a 5–0 win at Portsmouth in October 1955, was described in the press as being 'stunning', and Brown also scored three goals in a 7–1 FA Cup victory against Torquay in January 1956 to set Blues on the road to Wembley. However, he blamed himself for the 1956 Final defeat after missing two clear-cut chances and also failing to convert an early chance in the 1957 FA Cup semi-final against Manchester United, but all great strikers miss the target from time to time.

Brown formed a fine strike partnership in the Blues attack with inside-left Peter Murphy, who was also an ex-Coventry City player. He was quick over the ground, packed a fierce shot in his right foot and was also good in the air, but his main asset was his anticipation – and on several occasions he would dart into the penalty area to knock home a loose ball or deflect a low cross past the goalkeeper, often finding the net from an acute angle.

In January 1959 Brown finally left the Blues, having netted 90 goals in 185 first-class matches. He then played for Leyton Orient until the summer of 1961, and after a brief spell in non-League football with Scarborough and Stourbridge he took over as player-manager of Bedworth Town in 1963 and later assisted Wigan Athletic before announcing his retirement in December 1964, having struggled for some time with a knee injury.

At that juncture, Brown became a teacher and served as a games master for 10 years at Preston Catholic school – and one of his great achievements was to 'discover' the future Liverpool and Republic of Ireland defender Mark Lawrenson. Eddie now describes himself as sublimely retired and enjoys a round of golf twice a week.

Steve Bruce

Date of birth: 31 December 1960, Corbridge, Northumberland

Blues record:
Appearances: League 70+2, FA Cup 6, League Cup 6
Goals: League 2, FA Cup 1, League Cup 0
Debut: League, 18 August 1996 v Crystal Palace (h) won 1–0
Manager: December 2001–present

Also played for: Wallsend Lads' Club, Gillingham, Norwich City, Manchester United, Sheffield United, England (1 B cap)
Also managed: Sheffield United, Huddersfield Town, Wigan Athletic, Crystal Palace

Central-defender Steve Bruce scored 35 goals in 234 senior appearances for Gillingham (from August 1977), 20 in 180 for Norwich City (signed for £125,000 in August 1984) and 51 in 414 for Manchester United (signed for £800,000 in December 1987) before joining Blues on a free transfer in June 1996, at the age of 35.

A former shipyard worker in the north of England and an England Youth international (capped eight times), Bruce was voted Man of the Match in the 1985 League Cup Final when Norwich beat Sunderland and was a star performer when the Canaries won the Second Division title the following season. He skippered United on several occasions during his time at Old Trafford, helping the Reds win three Premiership titles, two FA Cup and two League Cup Finals, the European Cup-winners' Cup, the European Super Cup and two FA Charity Shields, while also collecting a handful of runners'-up prizes as well.

It was a crying shame that Bruce never gained a full England cap, his only other representative honours, apart from those he won as a Youth-team player, came via an appearance in a B international and an outing for the Football League representative side.

Bruce spent two seasons as a player with Blues, adding a further 84 senior appearances and two more goals to his tally before switching his allegiance north to Sheffield United, who signed him for £200,000, engaging him as their player-manager in June 1998.

When he finally retired as a player in early June 1999, Bruce had amassed almost 925 first-class appearances at club and international level, scoring 108 goals, his haul of 19 for Manchester United during the 1990–91 season being among the most ever netted by a defender in a season of top-class football. He took over as manager of another Yorkshire club, Huddersfield Town, in 1999, and he subsequently joined the board of directors at the Alfred McAlpine Stadium before leaving to work as a part-time coach at Nottingham Forest in 2000. He then returned to senior football management with Wigan Athletic, albeit briefly, early in 2001, prior to the appointment of Paul Jewell, and after a spell in the hot seat at Crystal Palace, from the summer of 2001, he was appointed as manager of Birmingham City, taking over in December 2001 from Trevor Francis who, by coincidence, was handed the vacant manager's job at Palace.

Bruce – admired by the players and by most of the die-hard Blues supporters – duly guided the team into the Premiership for the first time in the club's history in 2002 via a penalty shoot-out in the First Division Play-off Final at Cardiff's Millennium Stadium against his former club Norwich City, thus bringing top-flight football back to St Andrew's for the first time in 16 years. However, four years later, after a disappointing campaign on the back of a reasonable 2004–05 season when he lifted Blues to their highest League placing since 1977–78 (12th), the team were relegated.

Kenny Burns

Date of birth: 23 September 1953, Glasgow

Blues record:
Appearances: League 163+7, FA Cup 11, League Cup 12+2, others 9
Goals: League 45, FA Cup 3, League Cup 2, others 3
Debut: League, 1 September 1971 v Hull City (a) as substitute, lost 0–1

Also played for: Glasgow Rangers (schoolboy forms), Nottingham Forest, Leeds United, Derby County, Notts County, Barnsley, Elfsborg (Sweden), Sutton Town, Stafford Rangers, Grantham Town, Gainsborough Trinity, Ilkeston Town, Oakham United, Telford United, Scotland (2 Under-23, 20 full caps)

Scotsman Kenny Burns could play in any position and often did. Physically strong, he was a player feared by many. A powerful header of the ball, he tackled with purpose and aggression and could shoot with both feet. He started out as a dominant centre-half before becoming a very useful striker, scoring plenty of goals, and he also turned out in midfield, inside-forward, as an emergency full-back and occasionally as a winger. After leaving St Andrew's, he reverted back to a defensive role with Nottingham Forest.

Burns was on schoolboy forms at Ibrox Park before joining Birmingham City as an apprentice in the summer of 1970, turning professional the following year (July 1971). Staying at St Andrew's until July 1977, he amassed a fine record with Birmingham, scoring a goal every four games. He made a relatively slow start to his League career, making only eight appearances in his initial season in the first XI, that of 1971–72, when Blues gained promotion to the top flight as runners-up. The following season he was called into action 19 times, mainly occupying a midfield position, and scored his first goal for the club in a 3–2 defeat at Wolves, adding two more to his tally right at the end of the campaign, in home wins over relegated West Bromwich Albion and third-placed Leeds United.

Burns started 1973–74 as Roger Hynd's central-defensive partner, but, when striker Bob Latchford was transferred to Everton in the February, he was pushed into the centre-forward berth by his manager Freddie Goodwin, and what a fine job he did as leader of the attack. Having had to deal with some stocky, forthright strikers in his early days, he had no trouble whatsoever in matching the physical strength of the array of defenders who opposed him in his new role, and, in fact, he quickly settled down alongside Trevor Francis and Bob Hatton in the Blues attack, scoring five times before the end of the season, including a splendid hat-trick in a 3–3 draw at Leicester in early April.

Burns's form at this stage was impressive, and in March 1974 he gained the first of his 20 full caps for Scotland, lining up as strike partner to Denis Law in a 2–1 defeat by West Germany in Frankfurt. His other 19 international appearances followed between October 1974 and May 1981, playing in the 1978 World Cup Finals in Argentina. He also represented his country in two Under-23 matches against Wales and Holland in the mid–1970s.

Burns finished as second top scorer for Blues (behind Francis) in his last season at St Andrew's (1976–77), and his haul included another terrific hat-trick against Leicester, who were hammered 6–2 at Filbert Street in early December, and a four-timer in a 5–1 home win over Derby County two months earlier. Unfortunately, he failed to win any major prizes with Blues other than promotion, but, after moving to Nottingham Forest for £150,000 in July 1977 and reverting back to a defensive position, he helped Brian Clough's team win the European Cup twice in 1979 and 1980 and the First Division Championship and League Cup double in 1978, the same year he was voted PFA Footballer of the Year. He also played in the losing League Cup Final of 1980, and he certainly surprised his manager with his accomplished style.

In October 1981 – after almost 200 appearances for Forest – Burns moved to Leeds United for £400,000. Unfortunately, he was never the same player at Elland Road, where he partnered Paul Hart in defence, and in March 1984, after two separate loan spells with Derby County, he moved back to the East Midlands to sign for the Rams on a permanent basis.

At this juncture, Burns was getting a fraction slower, his reactions weren't quite so sharp and after a brief spell with Notts County (February–May 1985) Kenny appeared in his 424th and last Football League game as a non-contract player for Barnsley against Crystal Palace on 26 April 1986.

After a spell in Sweden, Burns toured the non-League scene before hanging up his boots in 1994 to become a publican, first in Ilkeston and later in Stoke-on-Trent.

Steve Claridge

Date of birth: 10 April 1966, Portsmouth

Blues record:
Appearances: League 86+2, FA Cup 7, League Cup 14+1, others 9+1
Goals: League 35, FA Cup 0, League Cup 2, others 5
Debut: League, 11 January 1994 v Notts County (a) lost 2–1

Also played for: Portsmouth (three spells), Fareham Town, Bournemouth, Weymouth (two spells), Basingstoke Town, Crystal Palace, Aldershot, Cambridge United (two spells), Luton Town, Leicester City, Millwall (two spells), Brighton & Hove Albion, Brentford, Wycombe Wanderers (two spells), Gillingham, Walsall, Bradford City
Managed: Weymouth (as player-manager), Portsmouth (as player-manager), Millwall

Footballing nomad Steve Claridge served with 17 different clubs over a period of 24 years, having his best spell with Blues, for whom he scored 42 goals in 120 appearances between January 1994 and March 1996. He was an apprentice at Fratton Park in 1982 but failed to make the grade and moved into non-League football a year later with Fareham Town. Taken on as a professional by Bournemouth in August 1984, he made his League debut against Gillingham in January 1985 and netted his first goal at that level against Newport County four months later.

Claridge was up and running, and he never stopped until 2006, amassing a superb record of more than 725 appearances and over 220 goals for his League clubs alone, while also starring in over 100 games at non-League level and striking another 30 goals.

Always seemingly scruffy with his socks rolled down to his ankles, wearing floppy shorts and at times a baggy shirt, Claridge's appearance belied his talent, for he was especially good on the ball and his stamina was second to none. He covered acres of ground during a game and often seemed to be moving faster at the end of a match than he did at the start. He was positive in his approach to a game, encouraged others around him and never gave less than 100 percent, and he was a great competitor who if he had been with a more fashionable club may well have gained representative honours.

Prior to joining Blues for £350,000, Claridge had helped Cambridge United win the Third Division Championship in 1991 and, in fact, was one of the most talked about and admired players in the lower Leagues for many years. He struck it rich with Blues in 1995, gaining two medals for winning the Second Division title and beating Carlisle United with a sudden-death goal in the Auto Windscreens Shield Final at Wembley. He averaged a goal every three games that season, despite having 13 different strike partners, and he was certainly a huge favourite with the fans – not only at St Andrew's but everywhere he played.

Claridge left Blues to join Leicester in a £1.2 million deal on the transfer deadline of 1996 and within a matter of weeks had helped them reach the Premiership by scoring a dramatic winning goal against Crystal Palace in the very last minute of extra-time in the First Division Play-off Final. A year later he struck again at Wembley, grabbing another extra-time winner as they beat Middlesbrough in the League Cup Final.

When almost 32, Claridge joined Wolves for £400,000 in March 1998, but he never fitted in at Molineux and moved back to Portsmouth for half that amount of money five months later. He later did a good job as manager of Weymouth but was in the hot seat at Millwall for only 37 days in June–July 2005.

Claridge was also notorious for a couple of off-the-field incidents. He was picked up by police for supposedly being drunk but, in fact, he was feeling ill after eating a full mixed grill and a couple of bars of chocolate in the space of half an hour. He loved to gamble, often being spotted inside a bookmaker's shop. However, that apart, he was a fine footballer, and he now works as a match summariser covering various football games on live TV.

Johnny Crosbie

Date of birth: 3 June 1896, Gorbals, Glasgow, Scotland
Died: 8 February 1992, Warwickshire

Blues record:
Appearances: League 409, FA Cup 23
Goals: League 71, FA Cup 1
Debut: League, 28 August 1920 v South Shields (a) lost 3–0

Also played for: Glenbuck Cherrypickers (Scotland), Muirkirk Athletic, Saltcoats Victoria, Ayr United, Chesterfield, Stourbridge (player-manager), Scotland (2 full, 1 Victory cap)

Inside-right John Anderson Crosbie was a superb creator of goals, and he contributed in no small measure to the impressive goal tally of Birmingham's great striker Joe Bradford. A genuine craftsman who could use both feet, his adept ball control and stratagems were delights to savour. He was a glutton for work, he was always involved in the action, could spray passes out to his colleagues with great precision up to 40 yards and even if the game itself was a dull affair he seemed to sparkle. He simply loved his football, and he certainly gave Blues tremendous service for over 12 years.

Crosbie started out in local non-League football in Scotland, joining his first professional club Ayr United in August 1913 at the age of 17. He played throughout World War One and represented Scotland in a Victory international against England in 1919 and earned his first full cap against Wales before joining Blues for a then record fee of £3,700 in May 1920. 'Too much, far too much' claimed one director, but he turned out to be real bargain, rated as one of Blues' finest investments.

In his first season at St Andrew's, Crosbie partnered 'Lol' Burkinshaw on the right-wing with Joe Lane at centre-forward and ex-Aston Villa hero Harry Hampton and Jack Whitehouse on the opposite flank. An ever present, he produced some quality performances, scored 14 goals and helped Blues win the Second Division Championship on goal average from Cardiff City. The following season he was joint top scorer with Joe Bradford on 10 goals, and he also collected his second full cap, starring in a 1–0 victory over England at Villa Park when the report in the *Daily Mirror* stated 'His passes were just about perfect.'

In seasons 1922–23 and 1923–24, Crosbie was on the score sheet just once each time, netting the winner at Preston in March in the former campaign and in a 4–1 home win over Newcastle in the latter. Yet despite his lack of marksmanship, his displays in centre-field were again impressive. Known as 'Peerless', his scoring form returned during the mid to late 1920s as Blues fought hard and long to get into the top half of the First Division table, and with a change in personnel things improved on the pitch, so much so that Blues reached the 1931 FA Cup Final where they met West Bromwich Albion. Crosbie worked tirelessly on a soggy Wembley pitch, but his efforts were in vain as the Blues lost 2–1. Johnny's pen-picture in the programme for that Cup Final read 'The master mind of the Birmingham attack... for Crosbie is a real star... Without Crosbie the Birmingham team would be sadly handicapped – it is fortunate for this unlucky club that Crosbie has escaped serious injury.'

In the summer of 1932 Crosbie, then 36 years of age, left St Andrew's to join Chesterfield, but he stayed at Saltergate barely four months before returning to the Midlands to become player-manager of Stourbridge. In February 1933 he accepted a six-month coaching position in Gothenburg, Sweden, and in 1934–35 ran a works team in Kidderminster. A button-maker by trade, he lived until he was 85 years of age.

Johnny lies in fifth place in Blues' greatest number of appearance makers – behind Gil Merrick (551), Frank Womack (515), Joe Bradford (445) and Ken Green (443). He is in seventh place in the club's list of greatest goalscorers.

Don Dearson

Date of birth: 13 May 1914, Ynysybwl near Pontypridd, Glamorgan
Died: 24 December 1990, Sheldon, Birmingham

Blues record:
Appearances: League 131, FA Cup 6, Wartime 166
Goals: League 17, FA Cup 0, Wartime 25
Debut: League, 15 December 1934 v Huddersfield Town (h) lost 4–0

Also played for: Llantwit Major Juniors, Barry Town, Northampton Town (guest), Nottingham Forest (guest), West Bromwich Albion (guest), Wrexham (guest), Coventry City, Walsall, Nuneaton Borough, Bilston United, Wales (4 amateur, 3 full and 15 wartime caps)

Football took second place for Don Dearson until he had completed his apprenticeship as an electrician. He played at weekends for Llantwit Juniors and then for Barry Town. When Aberaman were the visitors for a Welsh League match in 1933, scouts from several Football League clubs turned up to take a look at the home side's young and promising inside-forward and his counterpart, Bryn Jones of Aberaman. Birmingham City, Bristol City, Cardiff City, Huddersfield Town, Newport County, West Bromwich Albion and Wolves were all represented, and it was George Liddell, the Blues manager, who admired Don most of all, asking him to come to St Andrew's for a 'look round' and to play in a reserve-team match. Jones, incidentally, opted to join Wolves.

Dearson liked what he saw and accepted the offer made to him by Blues, who also arranged for his apprentice indentures to be transferred from the Aberthaw Cement Works to the Midland-based BSA factory. Once his apprenticeship was complete, he became a full-time professional, signing the appropriate papers in August 1934, and after four League outings that season (against Huddersfield Town, Sheffield Wednesday twice and Sunderland) and six the following season, when he also netted his first goal in a 4–3 defeat at Everton, he became a regular in the side in 1936–37, playing in 18 of the first 24 games before suffering from an ankle injury.

Blessed with an impressive physique, Dearson regained full fitness and his first-team place, and in February 1939 he played against Everton in a fifth-round FA Cup tie in front of the biggest-ever crowd at St Andrew's – 67,341. That same season he won three full caps for Wales – lining up against Scotland, Northern Ireland and France.

On the outbreak of World War Two, Dearson joined the Birmingham City Police Force but gave that up after just nine weeks and went to work for BSA on munitions, where he remained until 1948, although he did manage to play a lot of football during the hostilities, appearing in well over 160 games for Blues, guesting for four League clubs and gaining a record 15 wartime caps for his country (three goals scored). Then, in 1946, having been converted into a half-back, he helped Blues win the Football League South Championship and reach the FA Cup semi-final. He formed a wonderful middle line with Fred Harris and Arthur Turner and scored a crucial goal in the 2–2 League draw with Aston Villa in front of almost 64,000 fans at Villa Park in mid-January – and that point, technically, decided the title, Blues finishing ahead of their arch-rivals!

Dearson eventually left St Andrew's in February 1947 after 13 years' service, joining Coventry City for a fee of £6,000. After notching 11 goals in 88 games for the Sky Blues, he moved to nearby Walsall in March 1950 and then, after serving two non-League clubs, Nuneaton Borough and Bilston United, he announced his retirement in 1954 at the ripe old age of 40. He then ran his own grocery shop in Yardley, Birmingham, until 1967 when he sold up to take employment at the BSA works in Coventry. He and his sport-mad son attended St Andrew's quite regularly until his health started to deteriorate in the early 1980s.

Mark Dennis

Date of birth: 2 May 1961, Streatham, London

Blues record:
Appearances: League 130, FA Cup 7, League Cup 8
Goals: League 1, FA Cup 0, League Cup 0
Debut: League, 16 September 1978 v Norwich City (a) lost 4–0

Also played for: Chelsea Boys, Southampton, Queen's Park Rangers, Crystal Palace, Brighton & Hove Albion (trial), England
(3 Youth and 3 Under-21 caps)

One of the finest full-backs ever to play for Birmingham City, London-born Mark Earl Dennis would, one feels, have achieved far greater things if he had been able to control his fiery temper. He could be a real hot head and would fly off the handle at the slightest provocation. He was cautioned several times and sent off on at least 12 occasions during his 14-year career – but this lack of discipline should not overshadow his great ability as a left-sided defender. At times he was brilliant, and he knew it! Defensively alert and uncompromising, he gave the team an extra cutting edge with his superb overlaps down the left touchline. His enthusiasm and commitment made him very popular with the St Andrew's crowd, and he certainly enjoyed the big occasion. However, his disciplinary record saw him serve over a dozen suspensions, meaning he missed several crucial games, and his manager wasn't at all pleased.

Released as a youngster by Chelsea, Dennis joined Blues as an apprentice in June 1977 and turned professional in August 1978. After some purposeful displays in the second team, he made his senior Blues debut in rather unusual circumstances. Named in the Blues party to travel to Norwich for a League game in September 1978, he was suddenly asked to get changed by manager Jim Smith after right wing-back Jimmy Calderwood had slipped on the dressing room floor and cracked open his head. Unfortunately, it wasn't the greatest of starts to Dennis's career as the Canaries won 4–0. Putting that experience behind him, he worked hard at his game, and in his preferred left-back position he quickly gained a regular place in the side, making a total of 32 appearances that season in a struggling Blues side, which fell through the trapdoor and into the Second Division.

Undeterred, Dennis and his colleagues buckled down to business, and within 12 months Blues had regained their top-flight status by finishing third in the table, thanks mainly to a fine end-of-season run which saw them lose only one of their last nine games. Mark was absent only twice during the campaign, missing the 1–0 win at Charlton and the 3–3 home draw with Notts County on the final Saturday. He also gained the first of three England Under-21 caps that season against Bulgaria, and he played against Norway and Romania the following term. As a teenager, he had represented his country at Youth-team level.

After an impressive start to 1980–81, Dennis was injured in the home game with Crystal Palace in early November and took time to regain full fitness. He was out of action until March and the same sort of thing happened the following season. He was injured twice, and the second time it kept him out of the side from February to September 1982. In November 1983, after more injuries worries, he was transferred to Southampton for a cut-price of £30,000 (the original fee was set at £100,000). In his first season at The Dell he helped Saints reach the FA Cup semi-final and finish runners-up in Division One, but after a series of run-ins with new manager Chris Nicholl, he moved on to pastures new, this time Queen's Park Rangers. He spent one season at Loftus Road then three with his next club Crystal Palace before having an unsuccessful trial with Brighton.

Quitting competitive football in 1992, Mark moved to Spain where he now works as a signwriter.

Julian Dicks

Date of birth: 8 August 1968, Bristol

Blues record:
Appearances: League 83+6, FA Cup 5, League Cup 5, others 2
Goals: League 1, FA Cup 0, League Cup 0, others 0
Debut: League, 24 August 1985 v Chelsea (a) lost 2–0

Also played for: West Ham United (two spells), Liverpool, Canvey Island, England (2 B and 4 Under-21 caps)

Julian Andrew Dicks – nicknamed the 'Terminator' for his tenacity – was another exceptionally fine left-back who also drew up a terrible disciplinary record. He was sent off eight times during his career – five of his dismissals coming as a Hammers player and another when making his England Under-21 debut as a substitute versus Switzerland in 1988 – and he received over 40 yellow cards. He served Blues for three and a half years, making just over 100 first-class appearances.

Although born in Bristol, Dicks moved to Birmingham as a youngster and ended his educational studies at Washwood Heath School before joining the apprentice ranks at St Andrew's in August 1984, turning professional in August 1985, when he made his League debut as a 17-year-old substitute against Chelsea at Stamford Bridge, replacing David Geddes in the second half. Blues were relegated at the end of that season, Dicks having made a total of 26 senior appearances, six as a substitute.

The following season Dicks added 37 more outings to his tally, but once again Blues struggled desperately in the League, finishing 19th in Division Two, avoiding relegation by a mere two points. Having already been partnered with eight different full-backs in his first two seasons of senior football at St Andrew's, he started 1987–88 with the former Manchester City defender Ray Ranson on his right, and this seemed to be Blues' best pairing in front of goalkeeper Tony Godden. However, yet again, things didn't go at all right out on the pitch, and with Blues in deep trouble again, hovering around the relegation zone, he opted to leave Blues to sign for West Ham United for a fee of £400,000, the deal being completed on transfer deadline day in March. Blues managed to escape the drop that season while Dicks set off on a new career with the Hammers, who appointed him as team captain. He spent five and a half years at Upton Park, helping the London club gain promotion from the Second Division in 1991 while accumulating a further 203 senior appearances and netting 40 goals, the majority of which came from the penalty spot or from free-kicks 25–30 yards out. Yes indeed, he packed a powerful left-foot shot and always tended to blast his spot-kicks at goal, hardly ever missing from 12 yards.

From West Ham, Dicks joined Liverpool in a £2.5 million transaction in September 1993 – a deal sanctioned by manager Graeme Souness, which also included David Burrows and Mike Marsh. He made his debut in the Merseyside derby and remained at Anfield for 14 months, making a further 28 appearances before returning for a second spell with the Hammers after signing for £1 million. Unfortunately, he suffered a serious injury to his left knee in May 1997 but recovered and made a miraculous comeback in September 1998, only to break down again in April 1999, announcing his retirement at that point. He made a brief return in non-League football with Canvey Island in August 2000 but called it a day for good at the end of that season when he embarked on a new career in snooker – a game in which he did very well.

Dicks, whose playing credentials were never questioned, won two B and four Under-21 caps for England and was twice named as a reserve for the full international squad. He made 450 appearances at club and international level, netting a total of 64 goals, making him one of the highest-scoring full-backs of all time in senior football. His best haul in a season came in 1992–93 when he netted 11 times for West Ham (all in the League). He was voted Hammer of the Year on four occasions and had a benefit match against Athletic Bilbao in August 2000.

Neil Dougall

Date of birth: 7 November 1921, Falkirk, Scotland

Blues record:
Appearances: League 93, FA Cup 15, Wartime 38
Goals: League 15, FA Cup 3, Wartime 10
Debut: League South, 25 August 1945 v West Ham United (h) lost 1–0
Senior debut: FA Cup, 5 January 1946 v Portsmouth (h) won 1–0

Also played for: Burnley, Coventry City (guest), Oldham Athletic (guest), Walsall (guest), Plymouth Argyle, Scotland (1 full and 1 Victory cap)

Initially an inside-forward and later a resolute wing-half, Cornelius Dougall came from famous footballing stock – his father William played for Falkirk and Burnley and represented the Scottish League, while his uncle, James, served with Preston North End, Carlisle United, Halifax Town and was capped once by Scotland in 1939.

Dougall was a powerful red-head blessed with a terrific engine. He could and would play anywhere on the pitch to get a game, preferring a forward role until he was successfully switched to the middle line as the years rolled by. He joined Burnley as a 14-year-old, turned professional at Turf Moor in the summer of 1940 and played as a guest for Coventry City, Oldham and Walsall during World War Two. He also assisted Birmingham City in August and September 1945 before joining Blues on a permanent basis for £2,750 in October of that same year.

For the remainder of that season Dougall formed an excellent right-wing partnership with fellow Scot Jock Mulraney and helped Blues win the Football League South Championship, ahead of arch-rivals Aston Villa, Dougall scoring 10 goals in 38 appearances. He also represented Scotland in a Victory international against England in front of almost 139,500 spectators at Hampden Park in April 1946 and followed up six months later by gaining his only full cap against Wales at Wrexham. He also played for his country against England in the Bolton Disaster fund international of 1947.

Dougall weighed in with nine more League goals for Blues in 1946–47, but after that he didn't find the net all that often. He was, nevertheless, a vital cog in the team, linking together the midfield and attack with some shrewd and intelligent play. In 1947–48 he played superbly well as partner to first Jack Goodwin and then to another fellow countryman Jackie Stewart, as Blues went on to capture the Second Division title with an average home attendance of 36,467– the best in the club's history.

Dougall remained in the top flight of English football until March 1949 when he was transferred to Plymouth Argyle for a fee of £13,000, having scored 28 goals in 146 first-team matches for Blues. Plymouth knew they had recruited a specialist inside-forward, adding to their staff one of the most versatile footballers ever to don an Argyle shirt. He went on to score 26 goals in 289 first-class matches for the Pilgrims, helping them win the Third Division South title in 1952, and, after being successfully switched to right-half following an injury to George Taylor, before being pushed back into the forward line, he starred again when the Devon club clinched the Third Division Championship in 1959.

Retiring as a player in the summer of 1959, Dougall was appointed assistant trainer at Home Park, moving up to head trainer in rapid time. In March 1960 he was appointed joint manager of the Pilgrims with the aforementioned George Taylor, but this job proved difficult, and in June 1961 Taylor pulled out, allowing Dougall to run the team on his own, a job he held until the following November when he quit after seeing his team concede five goals in three successive League matches. He remained with the club as trainer and coach until March 1968 and, all told, he served Plymouth Argyle for almost 20 years, being a well-respected gentleman in the west country.

David Dunn

Date of birth: 27 December 1979, Great Harwood, Lancashire

Blues record:
Appearances: League 37+10, FA Cup 5+1, League Cup 2+2
Goals: League 6, FA Cup 1
Debut: League, 16 August 2003 v Tottenham Hotspur (h) won 1-0

Also played for: Blackburn Rovers, England (4 Youth, 1 full and 20 Under-21 caps)

David Dunn joined his first club Blackburn Rovers shortly after leaving school in the summer of 1995, and, after two years being nurtured through the youth, intermediate and reserve teams at Ewood Park, he was upgraded to the professional pay roll by manager Gordon Hodgson in September 1997. He moved along quickly after that, and over the next six years – injuries permitting – he scored 38 goals in 170 competitive appearances for the Lancashire club, while occupying a central-midfield position, from where, using his natural body strength, he displayed great tenacity and urgency. Always eager to be involved in the action, he tackled strongly and fairly, generally producing fine form, although he is not the most assiduous at tracking back. Nevertheless, he helped Rovers win the League Cup in 2002 and also represented England at Youth-team level before going on to gain 20 Under-21 caps, the first as a substitute against the Czech Republic in 1999 and his last versus Portugal three years later. He also gained his first full cap, also as a substitute, in a 1–1 draw with the Portuguese at Villa Park in September 2002.

In July 2003 Blues manager Steve Bruce contacted his counterpart at Ewood Park, Graeme Souness, and negotiated the £5.5 million transfer of Dunn to St Andrew's. And what an impact the midfielder made – scoring from the penalty spot on his debut to earn Blues a 1–0 home win over Tottenham Hotspur and doing likewise in his third game, which earned another victory at Newcastle.

Linking up with Welsh international Robbie Savage, Stephen Clemence and Damien Johnson, David fitted into Bruce's plans perfectly, his mesmerising runs, clever footwork and elusive movement giving his opponents plenty to think about. Initially he was used as a wide midfielder at St Andrew's but was also very effective in the role of a withdrawn striker.

Unfortunately, in his first season with Blues, Dunn tore a hamstring twice – the second time just eight minutes into a fifth-round FA Cup replay with Sunderland. This put him out of action until near the end of the Premiership programme, and his boss admitted afterwards that if he'd remained fit then there was no doubt that Birmingham's push towards a UEFA Cup place would have continued longer. In the end they finished 10th – their highest League placing since 1973.

Injuries struck Dunn again in 2004–05, his season being cut short owing to hamstring trouble. Eventually, he underwent surgery in an attempt to cure the problem once and for all. He made only 12 senior appearances and his absence was a major blow for the club. When he was in the side, playing mainly on the left, he produced some dynamic performances, his passing and interplay with Emile Heskey being very impressive and giving opposing defenders a lot of trouble. He scored two goals, helping earn a point from a 3–3 draw with his former club Blackburn at Ewood Park, while his second sewed up victory in the away Premiership game against arch-rivals Aston Villa in December.

Sadly for Dunn, and, indeed, for Birmingham City Football Club, injuries plagued him again in 2005–06, and it must be said that if he had been fully fit and in form then Blues might, just might, have escaped relegation from the Premiership. We shall never know.

George Edwards

Date of birth: 2 December 1920, Treherbert, Glamorgan, South Wales

Blues record:
Appearances: League 84, FA Cup 15, Wartime 38
Goals: League 9, FA Cup 0, Wartime 10
Debut: League South, 25 August 1945 v West Ham United (h) lost 1–0
Senior debut: FA Cup, 5 January 1946 v Portsmouth (h) won 1–0

Also played for: Kilgetty Juniors, Swansea Town (amateur), Coventry City (guest), Cardiff City and Wales (1 amateur, 1 wartime, 1 Victory and 12 senior caps)

Swansea Town discovered outside-left George Edwards playing with the local non-League side Kilgetty Juniors. He signed amateur forms for the Swans in May 1938 but managed only a couple of first-team appearances and won a cap for his country at amateur level, before World War Two intervened. At the time he was also studying at Swansea University, and he combined his studies with the occasional wartime game with the Swans. He was subsequently called up for service with the RAF, based at Wellesbourne, and immediately encountered Harry Storer, the Coventry City manager, when playing cricket for his camp team.

Edwards was asked to play as a guest for the Sky Blues, and he spent two seasons at Highfield Road (1943–44 and 1944–45), appearing in 58 regional games and scoring 11 goals. He was also capped by Wales in a wartime international against England in May 1945, and a month later he joined Birmingham City as a professional, making his debut in the Football League South at home to West Ham on 25 August when he partnered Harold Bodle on the left wing. His excellent form brought him another cap, this time in a Victory international against England at The Hawthorns, which the Welsh won 1–0, and soon afterwards he played against Scotland at Hampden Park.

Showing a combination of speed and skill with powerful left-footed shooting, Edwards's direct style made him a crowd pleaser. He made 48 appearances for Blues in 1945–46, helping them win the League South title, several of his 13 goals proving decisive. Two seasons later, after an exceptionally good 1946–47 campaign when Blues finished third in Division Two, he starred again the following term when promotion was gained to the top flight, Blues edging out Newcastle United for the title after an 11-match unbeaten run from mid-March to the end of the League programme. He also collected the first of his 12 full caps for Wales, taking the left-wing berth against Scotland in October 1946. His last would be awarded in November 1949, also against the Scots.

Edwards made only eight League appearances at the start of 1948–49 before being transferred, perhaps surprisingly, to Cardiff City for £12,000 in the middle of a cold December night. He served the Bluebirds splendidly for six years, gaining a Welsh Cup-winners' medal in 1951, a Second Division runners'-up medal 12 months later, and he represented the Welsh League on several occasions. Regarded as one of Cardiff's best ever left-wingers, he bowed out with 34 goals to his credit in 194 senior outings.

During his time with Cardiff, Edwards continued his thesis on the Pembrokeshire coalfields (which he had studied at University, gaining his MA degree – one of only a handful of footballers to receive this honour). On his retirement in May 1955 he joined an oil company in South Wales, but within three years he was back at Ninian Park as a director – a position he held until 1978. He also worked as a broadcaster for BBC Radio Wales and contributed to a Sunday newspaper. A regular supporter of football, he attended several games at Ninian Park right up until the millennium before ill-health and old age started to catch up with him.

George is one of the oldest former Blues players still alive today (in 2006).

Winston Foster

Date of birth: 1 November 1941, South Yardley, Birmingham

Blues record:
Appearances: League 151+1, FA Cup 10, League Cup 6, Europe 1
Goals: League 2, FA Cup 0, League Cup 0, Europe 0
Debut: League, 27 April 1961 v Burnley (h) lost 1–0

Also played for: Crewe Alexandra (loan), Plymouth Argyle, Chelmsford City, Bromsgrove Rovers

Born during World War Two, hence his patriotic Christian name, Winston Foster started out as a long-legged, awkward-looking full-back until an injury to centre-half Trevor Smith led to him switching to the middle of the defence, where he looked far more at ease, going on to appear in 170 senior games for the club.

A pupil at Church Road Junior and Cockshut Secondary Modern Schools, Foster represented the Birmingham County FA before joining Blues as a junior in the summer of 1955, taking amateur status a year later and eventually turning professional in November 1958 at the age of 17.

Despite several sound performances in the second team, Foster had to wait until April 1961 before making his League debut, taking over from England international Smith in a 1–0 defeat at the hands of reigning champions Burnley at St Andrew's, and he also played in the next game at Leicester. The following season he made 16 appearances, 12 of which were at right-back. One of those outings was in the first leg of the Inter Cities Fairs Cup Final at home to the Italian side AS Roma when, deputising for Smith at centre-half, he did a solid job as Blues were held to a 2–2 draw.

Owing to the form of Stan Lynn and then Brian Rushton at right-back and Smith at centre-half, Foster was handed only six first-team appearances in 1962–63, playing in the opening League Cup tie against Doncaster Rovers, which Blues won 5–0, setting them on the road to the Final where they defeated Aston Villa, with Foster watching from the sidelines as a reserve. The following season he managed just 14 senior starts – one as an emergency centre-forward against Stoke City in April – but in 1964–65 he finally gained a regular place in the first team, initially at right-half before taking over in the centre when Smith moved to Walsall. He appeared in every game and scored his first goal for the club to salvage a point from a 1–1 home draw with Sheffield United. Sadly his efforts were all in vain as Blues suffered relegated to the Second Division that season, going down in last place.

Foster, who by now had developed into a very competent and reliable defender, good in the air despite his height, was joined in defence by Terry Hennessey for the 1965–66 campaign, and the following season he had Malcolm Beard as his defensive aide until getting himself injured at Carlisle in late October (cartilage trouble). He struggled to regain full fitness and as a result missed out on a League Cup semi-final appearance as Blues lost over two legs to Third Division pacesetters Queen's Park Rangers. He was then confined to the reserves for the first part of the 1967–68 campaign, returning after Christmas as Blues set out on a wonderful FA Cup run, which ended disappointingly in another semi-final defeat, this time against West Bromwich Albion. At this stage in his career he was nearing a personal milestone in League football for Blues – his 150th appearance – and that came against Middlesbrough (away) in September 1968. He played in only two more games after that, and after a loan spell with Crewe Alexandra he was transferred to Plymouth Argyle in June 1969. He deputised for Fred Molyneux at Home Park and later assisted Chelmsford City (1971–72) and Bromsgrove Rovers, the latter as a player in 1972–73 and then as assistant manager in 1973–74.

John Frain

Date of birth: 8 October 1968, Yardley, Birmingham

Blues record:
Appearances: League 265+9, FA Cup 12, League Cup 28, others 22
Goals: League 23, FA Cup 0, League Cup 1, others 2
Debut: League, 12 April 1986 v Newcastle United (a) lost 4–1

Also played for: Northampton Town, Moor Green

John Frain gave Birmingham City Football Club close to 13 years' loyal and dedicated service, appearing in 337 first-class matches, scoring 26 goals and gaining a winners' medal for victory in the Final of the Leyland DAF Trophy at Wembley in 1991.

Frain attended and played for Holy Souls Primary and Archbishop Tysley Schools and represented Birmingham Boys before joining the apprentice ranks at St Andrew's in June 1984, signing a non-contract agreement in July 1985 and eventually turning professional in October 1986. He formed a very effective full-back partnership with Julian Dicks in Blues' youth team but failed to impress when given his chance in the first team. In fact, he looked nervous during his senior outings at the tail-end of the 1985–86 season when Blues were doomed to relegation from the First Division, and again when he was introduced to the action at a time when Blues were fighting to retain their Second Division status at the end of 1986–87.

Frain appeared in a total of six games in those two campaigns under managers Ron Saunders and then John Bond, and he scored his first goal in a 1–1 home draw with Reading in April 1987. He was given 15 outings in 1987–88 by new boss Garry Pendrey and the following season that figure was doubled as Blues, disappointingly, slipped into the Third Division for the first time in the club's history. But it was not the end of the world. Along with seasoned professionals and a few new faces, he buckled down to help the Blues climb the ladder again. In 1989–90, now established in the left-back position, he missed only eight League games, following up with 42 appearances in 1990–91 when he helped Blues go all the way to Wembley and win the Leyland DAF Trophy, beating Tranmere Rovers 3–2, when big John Gayle netted twice.

In 1991–92 Frain had a few outings in midfield as well as at full-back under manager Terry Cooper, and his experience and know-how went a long way in helping the team gain promotion from the Third Division. But it was tough going after that, and Blues, who finished 19th in the 'new' First Division in 1992–93, were demoted in 20th position in 1993–94.

At this stage Frain was feeling the strain, injuries interrupting his game longer than he had anticipated. He stuck in there, though, and made 11 appearances in 1994–95 but missed out on a second Wembley appearance as Blues beat Carlisle United with a sudden-death goal from Paul Tait in the Final of the Auto Windscreens Shield. He added 34 appearances to his tally over the next season and a half and was the club's longest-serving player when he finally left St Andrew's for pastures new, joining Northampton Town in January 1997. He remained a Cobbler until 2002, helping them win the Third Division Play-off Final against Swansea City in April 2000, soon after reaching the personal milestone of 500 League appearances.

One of the game's true professionals and referred to in some quarters as 'Mr Dependable', Frain retired from senior football in March 2006 after a series of hamstring injuries. He made a combined total of 579 appearances for Blues and Northampton, scoring 33 goals, and he is currently 15th in the list of greatest appearance makers for Blues.

Trevor Francis

Date of birth: 19 April 1954, Plymouth, Devon

Blues record:

Appearances:	League 278+2, FA Cup 21, League Cup 19, others 10
Goals:	League 118, FA Cup 6, League Cup 4, others 5
Debut:	League, 5 September 1970, substitute v Cardiff City (a) lost 2-0
Manager:	May 1996-2001

Also played for: Detroit Express (two spells), Nottingham Forest, Manchester City, Sampdoria, Atalanta, Glasgow Rangers, Queen's Park Rangers, Sheffield Wednesday, England (5 Under-23 and 52 full caps)

Also managed: Sheffield Wednesday, Queen's Park Rangers, Crystal Palace

Trevor Francis became Britain's first £1 million footballer when he joined Nottingham Forest for £975,000 + VAT and levy charges in February 1979, manager Brian Clough stating 'He'll be worth double that amount – you see!'

Blessed with electrifying pace, intricate ball skills, a powerful right-foot shot and amazing self-confidence, even from an early age, Francis joined Birmingham City as a youngster straight from school in Devon in July 1969 and turned professional at St Andrew's in April 1971 – having already made his mark in League football. Indeed, he scored 15 goals in his first 16 League games for Blues between September 1970 and March 1971, including four in the Second Division home encounter with Bolton Wanderers two months before his 17th birthday (on 20 February), a game Blues won 4-0.

Francis helped his colleagues gain promotion to the First Division the following season (1971–72) by claiming 12 goals in 39 starts, and even in the top flight he continued to produce the goods, although his goal-return wasn't half as good as it had been in previous seasons, a blistering 35-yarder against Blackpool being the pick of the bunch. Nevertheless, he was now firmly in the spotlight, and at the start of 1974–75 he whipped in 10 goals in double-quick time before an injury at Bramall Lane sidelined him for four months. He recovered and hit three more goals, helping Blues pull clear of relegation with four points to spare. He struck 18 goals in 1975–76, when once again Blues squeezed out of a hole at the foot of the table, top scored with 21 the following season and in 1977–78 registered his best-ever haul of 29, 25 coming in the First Division alone when he was an ever present. At this juncture, he was being monitored by several top clubs and it was inevitable that he would leave St Andrew's.

After scoring 133 goals in 329 first-class matches for Blues, Francis departed for the City Ground, having given the club magnificent service. The fans who once loved him were bitterly disappointed to lose such a star player. Trevor brought a breath of fresh air to the club, his penetrating high-speed runs causing the most experienced defenders all sorts of problems. No sooner had he arrived at the City Ground, he then netted the winning goal for Forest in the 1979 European Cup Final win over FF Malmo, and a year later he gained a Super Cup-winners' medal and a League Cup runners'-up medal but missed out on a second European Cup prize through injury. After that, he had a second spell in the NASL with Detroit, assisted Manchester City and spent five seasons in Italy with Sampdoria and Atalanta, gaining a Cup-winners' medal with the former in 1985. He then added a Scottish League Cup-winners' medal to his collection in 1988 with Glasgow Rangers and three years later, following his transfer to Sheffield Wednesday from Queen's Park Rangers, he starred in the Owl's Division Two promotion-winning side and received a League Cup-winners' medal as a non-playing sub. A year later he was player-manager at Hillsborough, and he collected a runners'-up medals in both the League Cup and FA Cup Finals.

Francis returned to St Andrew's as manager in May 1996, and during his five-year tenure he guided Blues to the First Division Play-offs three seasons running, losing each time, and he was also bitterly disappointed when Blues were defeated by Liverpool on penalties in the Final of the League Cup at Cardiff's Millennium Stadium in 2001. Trevor, who was replaced at St Andrew's by Steve Bruce, later had a spell in charge of Crystal Palace (2001–02 – taking over from Bruce) before becoming a TV soccer pundit.

The recipient of five Under-23 and 52 full caps for England (the latter gained between February 1977 and April 1986), Francis scored 225 goals in 752 appearances during a wonderful playing career.

Barry Fry

Date of birth: 7 April 1945, Bedford

Blues record:

Manager: December 1993–June 1996

Played for: Manchester United, Bolton Wanderers, Luton Town, Gravesend & Northfleet, Leyton Orient, Romford, Bedford Town, England Schoolboys

Also managed: Dunstable, Hillingdon Borough, Bedford Town, Barnet (two spells), Maidstone United, Southend United, Peterborough United

An inside-forward, capped by England Schoolboys, Barry Fry, who trained with the likes of George Best, Denis Law and Bobby Charlton with Manchester United, failed to make the grade at Old Trafford and only had a handful of senior appearances for his other two major clubs before drifting into non-League football with Gravesend & Northfleet in 1966, later becoming a legend at Bedford for his over-elaborate free-kicks!

As a manager, Fry guided Dunstable to runners'-up position in the Southern League North in 1974–75 but didn't achieve much when in charge of Hillingdon, Bedford, Maidstone or Barnet first-time round, but when he returned to the latter club for a second spell in July 1986 he had a lot of success, developing a struggling side with low attendances, battling to even exist as a football club, into a Football League outfit after winning the Vauxhall Conference in 1991. He introduced some quality players, got a plan going and saw gates increase ten-fold at Underhill. In Barnet's first season in Division Four they reached the Play-offs, but were beaten by Blackpool, and this led to a bust-up with the club's chairman Stan Flashman.

Fry and Flashman clashed for a second time when Barnet were brought before an FA commission for not keeping their books correctly in November 1992. The club received a hefty fine, and Fry and the supporters became very critical about the way that Flashman was running the club. Barry was then sacked, only to be reinstated within a week. However, despite all these internal problems, Barnet continued to play well on the pitch.

After seven years in charge, Fry quit as manager in April 1993, taking over the reins at Southend United, moving to St Andrew's eight months later (in place of Terry Cooper) when Blues were struggling at the wrong end of the First Division table. However, for all his efforts – and his experience – he couldn't turn things round, Blues suffering relegation at the end of the campaign, a run of 14 games without a win being the main problem!

During the close season Fry, friendly, enthusiastic and vibrant with a terrific personality, thought long and hard ahead of Second Division football, and in 1993–94, using no fewer than 41 players, switching and swapping his team around mainly due to injuries, Blues regained their First Division status in style, and they also won the Auto Windscreens Shield at Wembley, a crowd of 76,663 cheering Paul Tait's sudden-death goal against Carlisle United. The following season, 1995–96, it was reported that he made tentative enquiries about every footballer in the country, and he utilised 47 players in total, an all-time record for any club since League football started in 1888. However, Blues failed to do the business on the field, finishing 15th in the table. This didn't please the board of directors, and after fans also lost their patience Fry was dismissed just nine months after being given a 'vote of confidence' by his chairman.

Fry was appointed as manager of Peterborough United in May 1996, and four years later he took Posh to Wembley for the Third Division Play-off Final against Darlington, which ended in a 1–0 victory, this after seeing his previous club Barnet eliminated in the semi-finals. Amazingly he walked out of London Road immediately after that triumph, but walked back in 24 hours later, saying 'They all got it wrong, I misunderstood what was said.'

Talking about Blues' owner David Sullivan, he said 'he doesn't know a goal-line from a clothes-line.' After being dismissed by Blues, he left this message on his answerphone: 'Kristine (his wife) has gone shopping, and I've gone down the job centre looking for new employment.'

Paul Furlong

Date of birth: 1 October 1968, Wood Green, London

Blues record:
Appearances: League 104+7, FA Cup 5, League Cup 11+2, others 4
Goals: League 50, FA Cup 3, League Cup 3, others 0
Debut: League, 18 August 1996 v Crystal Palace (h) won 1–0

Also played for: Enfield, Coventry City, Watford, Chelsea, Queen's Park Rangers, Sheffield United (loan), England (5 semi-professional caps)

Paul Furlong gained five semi-professional caps for England and helped Enfield win the FA Trophy in 1988 before moving out of non-League football in July 1991 at the age of 20 to join First Division Coventry City for £130,000. Over the next 15 years he scored more than 180 goals in nearly 550 competitive appearances, having by far his best spell with Birmingham City, whom he served for six years from July 1996 until August 2002.

A strong, purposeful, all-action striker, aggressive with good pace and powerful right-foot shot, Furlong had an excellent season with Coventry City before spending two years with Watford (signed for £250,000 in July 1992), followed by two more at Chelsea (secured for £2.3 million in May 1994). He was signed for Blues by manager Trevor Francis for £1.5 million and netted the 100th goal of his career during his time at St Andrew's, where he became a firm favourite with the fans.

Furlong appeared in 43 out of 46 League games for Blues during the 1996–97 season, notching 10 goals. His strike partners were Mike Newell and Paul Devlin, and between them their efforts, plus those of others, took Blues up to 10th place in the First Division and to the fifth round of the FA Cup.

For the 1997–98 campaign Peter Ndlovu was introduced to the attack, and he and Furlong developed a fine understanding with each other, netting a combined total of 30 goals, Paul top scoring with 19 including three penalties as Blues edged up to seventh in the table, missing out on the Play-offs on goal-difference to Sheffield United after failing to beat Charlton Athletic at home on the final day of the League programme. Disappointed, of course, Furlong and his teammates rolled up their sleeves and boldly set out on another attempt to win promotion in 1998–99. This time they claimed fourth place in the Division, qualified for the Play-offs and fancied themselves to reach the Premiership, only to lose in the semi-final 7–6 on penalties to his former club Watford after a 1–1 aggregate draw. By this time his strike partner in the Blues attack was Dele Adebola, and between them they notched 29 goals, both players grabbing 13 in the League.

The following season Furlong again top scored with 11 goals as Blues once more missed out on the Play-offs, losing 5–2 on aggregate to Barnsley, having finished fifth in the First Division, 12 points off an automatic promotion place. It was becoming hard and, indeed, frustrating, for all the players at St Andrew's – getting so near yet so far to earning a place in the top flight, and there was more agony for Furlong and his colleagues in 2000–01 as Blues, for the third time running, failed to make it through to the Final of the Play-offs, losing in the semi-finals to Preston North End 4–2 on penalties. Perhaps it wasn't as hard to take this time round for him, as he spent a loan spell with QPR – but nevertheless it was disappointment once more for the big man.

After this Furlong struggled to hold down a place in Blues' first team, and after assisting Sheffield United (on loan) he signed permanently for QPR in August 2002. He found his shooting boots and his form at Loftus Road and scored regularly for the London club, receiving the fans' Player of the Year, Players' Player of the Year and Goal of the Season awards in 2004–05, while at the same time making his 500th club appearance as a full-time professional.

Joe Gallagher

Date of birth: 11 January 1955, Liverpool

Blues record:
Appearances: League 281+5, FA Cup 21, League Cup 17, others 11
Goals: League 17, FA Cup 2, League Cup 4, others 0
Debut: Texaco Cup, 19 September 1973 v Stoke City (h) drew 0–0

Also played for: Rovaniemen Palloseura (Finland), Wolverhampton Wanderers, West Ham United, Burnley, Halifax Town, Padiham, Kings Heath, England (1 B cap)
Managed: Coleshill Town, Atherstone United, Kings Heath

Joe Gallagher recovered from three cartilage operations to take over at centre-half from Roger Hynd at the heart of the Blues defence in 1974, having previously occupied both full-back positions and the centre-forward berth. Tall and commanding, strong in the air and stylish on the ground, he went on to make 335 senior appearances for the club while also scoring his fair share of goals, and he was certainly unlucky not to gain a full international cap for England, one B team outing, against Australia on his home ground (St Andrew's) in 1980, proving to be his only representative honour.

Born in Liverpool, Gallagher joined Blues as an apprentice in July 1970 and turned professional on his 17th birthday, making his senior debut in a Texaco Cup tie against Stoke City in September 1973, with his Football League baptism following soon afterwards against Arsenal at Highbury when he did well marking John Radford. He made 35 senior appearances that season, scoring two goals, the first in a 3–1 home win in the return game against the Gunners and the second, the winner, at home to Manchester United in mid-March. The following season he added a further 50 outings to his tally and helped Blues reach the semi-finals of the FA Cup, but he was bitterly disappointed when Fulham went through to Wembley after winning the replay with a late goal in extra-time. His 100th appearance for the club came against Leeds United at St Andrew's in October 1975 and his 200th followed against Derby County in a fourth-round FA Cup tie in February 1978.

At that point – having got back into the side after an absence of more than four months, during which time he was recovering from a broken leg, sustained in a car crash, and regaining his fitness by playing in Finland – Gallagher was being accompanied in the centre of the Blues defence by Pat Howard, and in 1978–79 his partners included Garry Pendrey, Malcolm Page and Tony Want. However, that was the problem this term – an unsettled defence – which resulted in Blues being relegated to the Second Division.

Gallagher and his teammates, obviously disappointed at what had happened, bounced back quickly, gaining promotion at the first attempt under manager Jim Smith. He now had Colin Todd as his defence aide and had a superb season, missing only one League game. He also played well in 1980–81, but this was to be his last season with Blues, and to many people his £350,000 transfer to neighbouring Wolverhampton Wanderers came as a huge shock as he admitted that he loved Birmingham City. He was sold to the Molineux club so that hard-up Blues could cash in. He turned down a handful of approaches from other clubs before agreeing to join Wolves. However, he never settled in the Black Country and in December 1982, after just 34 outings for Wolves, he switched his allegiance to West Ham United, for whom he made 11 appearances. From August 1983 he served with Burnley (58 games) and went on to assist both Halifax Town and Padiham in the North-West Counties League on loan before quitting top-class football to take the position of manager with Coleshill Town, later holding similar positions with two other non-League teams, Atherstone United and Kings Heath. He was also engaged as Community officer by Blues during the early 1990s.

Joe made well over 400 appearances during his professional career – 377 in the Football League.

Archie Gemmill

Date of birth: 24 March 1947, Paisley, Scotland

Blues record:

Appearances: League 97, FA Cup 7, League Cup 10, other 1
Goals: League 12, FA Cup 1, League Cup 1, other 0
Debut: League, 18 August 1979 v Fulham (h) lost 4–3

Also played for: Drumpchapel Amateurs, St Mirren, Preston North End, Derby County (two spells), Nottingham Forest, Jacksonville Teamen (NASL), Wigan Athletic, Scotland (1 Under-23 and 43 full caps)
Managed: Rotherham United (joint, with John McGovern)

Midfielder Archie Gemmill, scorer of one of the finest individual goals in the Finals of World Cup football for Scotland against Holland in Argentina in 1978, had a wonderful career that spanned 20 years.

After being nurtured along in the Drumpchapel Amateurs side, Gemmill joined St Mirren in 1964, being Scotland's first-ever substitute when he came off the bench against Clyde in August 1966. In May 1967 he entered the Football League with Preston North End, manager Jimmy Milne paying £13,000 for his signature, beating off the challenge of several other English clubs.

A little over three years later, in September 1970, Gemmill joined Brian Clough's Derby County side for £66,000, and he spent seven years at the Baseball Ground before teaming up again with Clough at Nottingham Forest in September 1977, switching to Birmingham City for £150,000 in August 1979. In March 1982 he signed a five-month deal with the NASL club Jacksonville Teamen, re-entering the Football League with Wigan Athletic in September 1982 and later returning to Derby County in November 1982 to May 1984.

A short, stocky, 5ft 5ins tall, all-action, dynamic and sometimes aggressive player, Gemmill gained three League Championship-winning medals: two with Derby (1972 and 1975) and one with Forest (1978). He also won the League Cup and European Cup double with the latter club in 1979 and helped Blues gain promotion from the Second Division in 1980. He won one Under-23 and 43 full caps for Scotland over a period of 10 years (the last 10 as a Blues player). He gained his first in February 1971 against Belgium and his last in March 1981 against Northern Ireland. He also scored eight senior goals.

Signed by Blues manager Jim Smith following relegation from the top flight at the end of the 1979–80 season, Gemmill joined Alan Ainscow, Alan Curbishley and Kevin Dillon in the midfield engine room, and he produced some superb displays while scoring some vitally important goals in the process. He appeared in 37 League games in 1980–81, helping Blues finish third in the table and so regain their place in Division One at the first attempt. Five of his goals sealed victories over Queen's Park Rangers, Oldham Athletic, Swansea City and Watford at home and Charlton Athletic away. He also fired home a penalty in a 2–2 draw with his former club Preston.

The following season Gemmill missed only one game (a 2–2 draw at West Bromwich Albion), but two-thirds of the way through 1981–82, with the team fighting for points in mid-table, Archie, who had been struggling with a niggling knee injury, signed for the North American Soccer League club Jacksonville Teamen. He had given Blues excellent service, and the fans appreciated his hard work in helping the team regain its First Division status.

On retiring from playing Gemmill was appointed coach at his former club Forest (June 1984) and was manager of the second team for a short while before becoming joint manager of Rotherham United, with his former playing colleague John McGovern, in September 1994, retaining his position for two years.

Gemmill's career realised more than 650 League appearances north and south of the border (324 in two spells with Derby). His first game as joint manager of Rotherham was against Blues at Millmoor in September 1994, the final score being 1–1.

Alex Govan

Date of birth: 16 June 1929, Glasgow

Blues record:
Appearances: League 166, FA Cup 16, Europe 5
Goals: League 53, FA Cup 5, Europe 2
Debut: League, 19 August 1953 v Hull City (h) won 2–0

Also played for: Plymouth Argyle (two spells), Portsmouth

Alex Govan was a wonderful left-winger, industrious, fast and tricky, who regularly pushed the ball past his opponent, beating him for pace before getting in a dangerous cross. He wasn't a big man by any means, but, nevertheless, he was never completely mastered by the burly defenders who marked him, and quite often there were two opponents blocking his way to goal!

Despite being born in Scotland and playing for the Bridgton Boys Club (Glasgow), Govan started his League career with Plymouth Argyle. He was in the same team as Len Boyd and Gordon Astall at Home Park, and later all three players linked up with Birmingham City and helped Blues win the Second Division Championship in 1955 and reach the FA Cup Final the following season.

A consistent scorer throughout his career, Govan netted 38 goals in 150 appearances in two spells with Plymouth, helping them win the Third Division South title in 1952 and the Third Division Championship in 1959. He averaged a goal every three games for Blues, netting 60 times in 186 starts. Signed for £6,500 in June 1953 to replace Billy Wardle on Blues' left wing, he scored on his debut in a 2–0 win over Hull City on the opening day of the 1953–54 campaign and ended up with eight goals to his credit that season, following on with 16 in all games in 1954–55, playing a major part in bringing the Second Division trophy to St Andrew's. Indeed, he missed only five League games, through injury, and was quite brilliant in resounding home victories over Port Vale (7–2), Liverpool (9–1) and Ipswich Town (4–0). He also teased and tormented his markers in the 5–2 win at Middlesbrough and the 5–1 triumph at Doncaster on the final day of the season when the Championship was decided.

Unfortunately, Govan had a lean time in his first season in the top flight (1955–56), netting only four goals, and was bitterly disappointed not to have scored from the two chances he got in the 3–1 Cup Final defeat by Manchester City. That over and forgotten, he bounced back in style in 1956–57 and set a new Birmingham City club record for a winger by netting 30 goals in all competitions. In fact, he was the last player to reach this total in a season for the Midlands club. His tally also included five hat-tricks – four in the League against Portsmouth (away, won 4–3), Newcastle United (home, won 6–1), Preston North End (home, won 3–0) and Leeds United (home, won 6–2) and one in the FA Cup at Southend United (won 6–1). He actually claimed three trebles in four games in the space of 10 days. He was, however, sorry not to have reached a second FA Cup Final, Blues losing 2–0 to Manchester United in the semi-final of 1957 at Hillsborough.

Govan played in Blues' first-ever game in Europe against Inter Milan in the Inter Cities Fairs Cup 10 days after the 1956 Cup Final. They reached the semi-final of that competition but lost to Barcelona after a replay. It was around this time that he was in line for a call up to the Scottish national team, but with Tommy Ring, Tommy Ewing and Stuart Imlach all competing for the outside-left berth he missed out and was never in the frame again.

After playing in 17 of the first 20 games of 1957–58, Govan started to show signs of slowing down, and with Astall being switched to the left to accommodate Harry Hooper, he was pushed into the reserves. Eventually transferred to Portsmouth in March 1958, at the end of that season he returned to Plymouth, announcing his retirement in May 1960. He now resides at Hartley Vale near Plymouth and still follows football on TV.

Colin Green

Date of birth: 10 February 1942, Brynteg near Wrexham

Blues record:
Appearances: League 183, FA Cup 19, League Cup 15
Goals: League 1, FA Cup 0, League Cup 0
Debut: League, 15 December 1962 v Tottenham Hotspur (h) lost 2–0

Also played for: Everton, Wrexham, Tamworth, Rhyl, Wales (seven Under-23 and 15 full caps)

When left-back Colin Green made his Football League debut as a 17-year-old for Everton against Blackpool in September 1960, his opponent for most of the game was the legendary England winger Stanley Matthews. Nevertheless, he came through with flying colours and helped the Merseysiders win 4–1 in front of almost 25,000 spectators.

Exceptionally good on the overlap, Green was also extremely quick in recovery. He was a strong and forceful tackler, ice cool under pressure, defended resolutely and turned out to be one of Birmingham City's finest post-war full-backs, following his bargain £15,000 transfer fee, moving from Goodison Park to St Andrew's in December 1962. A bad knee injury, which came back to haunt him in later years, had severely restricted his progress at Everton, for whom he made just 18 appearances, but when Terry Hennessey, his pal and former school mate and future Welsh international colleague, recommended him to St Andrew's, Blues manager Gil Merrick had no second thoughts about signing the Welshman, the deal going through in double-quick time. In fact, he actually signed the appropriate forms inside an Aberdeen hotel when on duty with the Welsh Under-23 team.

Despite having a long line of partners at full-back, among them Stan Lynn, England international Bobby Thomson, Ray Martin and the ex-Chelsea star Bert Murray, Green drew up a fine understanding with them all. Without doubt, he was a very consistent performer who went on to appear in more than 200 competitive games for Blues, scoring just one goal – that being the winner in a 3–2 Second Division victory at Carlisle in September 1968. He also gained a League Cup-winners' tankard when Blues beat arch-rivals Aston Villa 3–1 in the two-leg Final of 1963, Colin keeping a tight grip on winger Alan Baker in both encounters, even finding time to venture forward and fire in two shots in the first leg at St Andrew's.

Green, who took over the left-back position at Blues from Graham Sissons, held his place, virtually unchallenged, until 1969, although injuries (which included a broken leg, twisted ankle, damaged knee, back trouble and disjointed toe), illness (a lengthy chest infection and flu) and international call-ups cut deep into his overall total of appearances. His longest run in the first team at League level was 37 matches from August 1966 to April 1967, and when he moved on in 1971 the number-three shirt went to the aforementioned Martin, who retained it on and off until 1976.

Green gained 15 full caps for Wales, the first against Italy in Florence in May 1965 when he partnered Graham Williams. His last senior appearance for his country was as a second-half substitute versus Northern Ireland in Belfast four years later, the game ending all square at 0–0. In May 1966, six months after breaking his leg in the League clash with Bristol City at Ashton Gate, he marked Brazil's flying winger Garincha in front of almost 160,000 fans in Rio's giant Maracana Stadium. He played well, and although Wales lost the game 3–1 this was one of the highlights of his professional career.

After a loan spell with Wrexham in January 1971, Green was released by Blues manager Freddie Goodwin at the end of that season. He quickly entered non-League soccer with Tamworth and after assisting Rhyl for a year he reluctantly announced his retirement in the summer of 1974 (mainly due to ill health) to concentrate on his garage business in North Wales. He later became a sales representative.

Ken Green

Date of birth: 27 April 1924, West Ham, London
Died: 10 June 2001, Sutton Coldfield

Blues record:
Appearances: League 401, FA Cup 35, European 6
Goals: League 3, FA Cup 0, European 0
Debut: League, 13 September 1947 v Brentford (a) won 2–1

Also played for: Millwall (amateur), England (2 B caps)

Ken 'Slasher' Green was one of the most durable defenders in League football between 1948 and 1958. A canny full-back, he shared in most of Blues' successes during the immediate post-war period and played in the 1956 FA Cup Final defeat by Manchester City. He formed excellent partnerships with first Dennis Jennings, then Jack Badham and finally with England international Jeff Hall. In fact, he and Hall played together in almost 190 senior matches for Blues between August 1951 and November 1958.

Brought up and educated in London, Green was on Millwall's books as an amateur before joining Blues as a professional in November 1943 at the age of 17. He was serving in the Army when he wrote to the secretary at St Andrew's asking for a trial, and he subsequently received a favourable return letter in the post, kept his appointment, showed up for his trial, impressed those watching and was immediately offered a contract in, of all places, the dressing room at Villa Park! He served overseas in the forces for quite some time before returning to England, but once he had bedded himself in at St Andrew's he worked hard at his game, and after some fine displays in the reserves he made an impressive League debut against Brentford, taking over at right-back from Cyril Trigg, who was switched into the forward line at a time when injuries were causing manager Harry Storer some concern.

Green took to competitive League football like a duck to water. He became an established member of Blues' first team during the 1947–48 season, appearing in 35 games and collecting a Second Division Championship-winners' medal in the process. Confident and totally committed, he continued to perform exceedingly well in the right-back position, and was unchallenged for five years before he switched to the opposite flank to accommodate the fast-improving Jeff Hall.

Thereafter, Green became an inspirational defender, producing some terrific displays and captaining the side on several occasions. His performances were certainly appreciated by the St Andrew's supporters. Although described in some quarters as being a stern tackler, he was never erratic in his challenges and always tried to jockey his opponent into a false sense of security by shepherding him close to the touchline. Very few wingers got the better of him, and those who did included the Chelsea outside-right Eric Parsons, Johnny Hancocks of Wolves and Tom Finney of Preston North End. He admitted that he enjoyed playing against Stanley Matthews, who was fast over the ground – for Green himself was no slouch when it came to pace, especially over 20–25 yards. He could match the quickest in the game from a standing start.

After his exploits in 1947–48, Green added a second League Division Two-winners' medal to his collection in 1955 and gained two caps for England B (v Yugoslavia and Switzerland in 1953–54) while also representing the Football League on two occasions against the Scottish League in 1952–53 and the Irish League the following season.

After appearing in more than 440 senior games for Blues, including the club's first in a major European competition versus Inter Milan (away) in the Inter Cities Fairs Cup in May 1956, he finally called it a day by announcing his retirement in the summer of 1959.

Green remained in Birmingham and later took over a post office on Oxhill Road, Handsworth, while at the same time remaining an ardent (and sometimes critical) Blues supporter until his death at the age of 77.

Jimmy Greenhoff

Date of birth: 19 June 1946, Barnsley, Yorkshire

Blues record:
Appearances: League 31, FA Cup 5
Goals: League 14, FA Cup 1
Debut: League, 31 August 1968 v Preston North End (a) lost 4-1

Also played for: Leeds United, Stoke City, Manchester United, Crewe Alexandra, Toronto Blizzard (NASL), Rochdale, Port Vale, England (1 B and 5 Under-23 caps)
Managed: Rochdale, Port Vale

Jimmy Greenhoff scored in two FA Cup semi-finals for different clubs on the same ground (Goodison Park). His first strike was for Stoke City against Arsenal in 1972 and his second for Manchester United against Liverpool seven years later. He also netted in another semi-final for Manchester United against his former club Leeds United at Hillsborough in 1977, going on to claim United's fortuitous winner in the Final of that year against Liverpool when future Blues manager Lou Macari's effort rebounded off his body and past the helpless Ray Clemence. He returned to Wembley two years later, but this time collected a runners'-up medal when Arsenal pipped United 3-2 with a last-minute goal from Alan Sunderland.

Previously a League Cup and Inter Cities Fairs Cup winner with Leeds, as well as gaining a runners'-up medal in the latter competition with the same club, Greenhoff helped Stoke beat Chelsea 2-1 in the 1972 League Cup Final, and he also represented the Football League and played once for England B and five times for the Under-23 side, but a full cap eluded him, despite his consistent performances and being rated as one of his country's finest strikers.

Greenhoff is listed in this book of legends simply because he was a class player – a quality inside-forward, adept at screening the ball with his back to goal and defender (or defenders) behind him, he was a clever footballer, very talented, packed a tremendous right-foot shot, was powerful in the air and scored some cracking goals in his time, some of them sweetly-struck volleys from just inside or outside the penalty area.

A Yorkshireman, and brother of Brian who also played for Leeds and Manchester United, Greenhoff helped Barnsley and Yorkshire Boys win the English Schools Trophy before becoming an apprentice at Elland Road in 1961, turning professional in August 1963. Unable to command a regular place in the first team at Elland Road, he was transferred to Blues for £70,000 in August 1968, signed by manager Stan Cullis in the middle of Leeds United's two-leg Fairs Cup Final against Ferencvaros.

After scoring on his debut for Blues, Greenhoff went on to claim 11 goals in his first 10 League outings, including a brilliant four-timer, and missed a penalty against Fulham in October 1968 when Blues won a thrilling contest 5-4. Unfortunately for him, the local and national press and local gossip soon made it apparent that Second Division Blues would not be able to retain his services, and after spending just 12 months at St Andrew's, in a deal shrouded in mystery, he was sold to Stoke City for £100,000. He went on to score 97 goals in 338 games for the Potters (including Goal of the Season against Blues at St Andrew's shortly after he had left) before adding 36 more to his tally in 122 outings for Manchester United.

As time went by Greenhoff moved down the League ladder, playing for Crewe Alexandra from December 1980 until May 1984, spending a few months as player-manager at Gresty Road. He then tried his luck in the NASL with Toronto Blizzard, joined Port Vale in August 1981 and became player-manager of Rochdale in March 1983. He returned to Vale Park in the same capacity in May 1984, later taking over as head coach, and finally quit football in the summer of 1985 to concentrate on coaching youngsters at holiday camps, which he combined with his main job as an insurance broker, based in Stoke-on-Trent.

Jimmy later developed his own business, Greenhoff Peutz and Co, based in Audley, Staffordshire, and he also worked briefly for a Staffordshire paint company.

Jeff Hall

Date of birth: 7 September 1929, Scunthorpe
Died: 4 April 1959, Birmingham

Blues record:
Appearances: League 227, FA Cup 33, Europe 5
Goals: League 1, FA Cup 0, Europe 0
Debut: League, 20 January 1951 v Bury (home) drew 3–3

Also played for: Bradford Park Avenue (amateur), England (1 B and 17 full caps)

Despite being on the small side, Jeff Hall was a wonderfully consistent right-back, highly efficient and durable with a first-rate temperament. His positional sense was superb, his tackling precise, and above all he was game to the last and very few wingers got the better of him. He was an England international who starred in 17 consecutive games for his country in exactly two years, from October 1955 until October 1957 when he lost his place to West Bromwich Albion's Don Howe.

Hall was a very perky sort of player, strong and enthusiastic and a fighter to the last. He played for several local junior teams including St Anne's, Wilsden and Top Bank before signing amateur forms with Bradford Park Avenue in August 1949. He completed his national service and joined Blues as a professional in May 1950. He developed in the second team before taking over the number-two shirt at St Andrew's halfway through the 1952–53 season, when Ken Green, who was to become a splendid full-back partner, moved across to the left flank. He retained his position competently thereafter, injuries and international duties apart, until he was tragically struck down with polio shortly after what was to be his last League appearance for Blues at Portsmouth in March 1959. He was only 29 years of age – and his demise proved to be a huge loss to Birmingham City, his only major club, and of course to English football in general.

Hall was a member of Blues' Second Division Championship-winning side of 1954–55, making 32 League appearances, all in succession, from early October, and 12 months later he played at Wembley in the FA Cup Final defeat by Manchester City. He wasn't at his best that afternoon, having struggled with a virus right up until the morning of the game. Five months after that Cup Final disappointment, he won his first full England cap, starring in a 5–1 win over Denmark in Copenhagen, and four weeks later he returned to Wembley to help his country beat Northern Ireland 3–0.

Roger Byrne, the Manchester United captain, was Hall's international full-back partner in each of his 17 senior appearances for his country, and England suffered only one defeat when Jeff was in the team, beaten 2–1 by Wales at Cardiff in his second outing. His B cap was won against West Germany in 1954–55, and he also represented Young England (against England in 1958), played for the Football League on four occasions (1955–57) and appeared twice for the FA when touring the West Indies in the summer of 1955.

During the 1955–56, 1956–57 and 1957–58 seasons, and for two-thirds of the 1958–59 campaign, Hall's form was outstanding, and he helped Blues finish sixth, 12th and 13th in the First Division. They also came mighty close to reaching their second FA Cup Final in two years. But unfortunately, with the possibility of an all-Midland (even Birmingham) Final, with Aston Villa playing West Bromwich Albion in the other semi, Blues went down 2–0 to Manchester United in the 1957 semi-final clash at Hillsborough. And there was another disappointment for him when Barcelona defeated Blues in the semi-final of the Inter Cities Fairs Cup, the Spaniards winning the replay 2–1 in Basle, Switzerland, after a 4–4 aggregate score over two legs.

Hall scored only one senior goal for Blues, and it came in the League game at Stoke in mid-September 1953 when he was pushed forward by manager Arthur Turner into the outside-right position after Scotsman Jackie Stewart had pulled out with an injury. Sadly, it was to no avail, as the Potters won 3–2.

Hall died just a fortnight after making the last of his 265 senior appearances for the club and it took everyone quite a while to recover from that devastating blow. A quiet, sombre crowd of just under 30,000 attended Blues home game with Bolton Wanderers four days after.

Harry Hampton

Date of birth: 21 April 1885, Wellington, Shropshire
Died: 15 March 1963, Wrexham, North Wales

Blues record:

Appearances: League 57, FA Cup 2, Wartime 1
Goals: League 31, FA Cup 0, Wartime 0
Debut: League, 14 February 1920 v Barnsley (a) won 5–0

Also played for: Potters Bank, Lilleshall Ironworks, Shifnal Juniors, Hadley FC, Wellington Town (two spells), Aston Villa, Newport County, Lilleshall Town, also guest during World War One for Bellis & Morcom FC, Blackpool, Derby County, Fulham, Nottingham Forest, Reading and Stoke, England (4 caps)

Although centre-forward Harry Hampson made his name and his mark as a goalscorer with Blues' arch-rivals Aston Villa, he nevertheless did an excellent job during his two and a half years at St Andrew's.

Known affectionately as 'Appy 'Arry' Hampton', he was a real terror to opposing goalkeepers and defenders alike, and during the decade leading up to World War One he was rated as one of the finest marksmen in Britain. Afraid of no one, his strong, forceful, determined style was admired and appreciated by plenty. The idol of the Villa Park faithful, Harry was robust to the extreme and often barged into an opposing goalkeeper, once knocking over Willie 'Fatty' Foulke, the giant 22-stone Sheffield United custodian. Quite regularly a defender had to pick himself up, gather his breath and dust himself down after being on the receiving end of one of his shoulder charges!

With a devil-may-care attitude, Hampton rattled in 242 goals in 376 senior games for Aston Villa, whom he served from August 1904 until February 1920 when he moved across the city to St Andrew's on a free transfer. He helped Villa twice win the FA Cup – in 1905 when he scored twice in the Final against Newcastle United and again in 1913 versus Sunderland. He also gained a League Championship-winners' medal in 1910 when he top scored with 26 First Division goals, including four hat-tricks.

Hampton represented England four times, scoring on his debut in a 4–3 win over Wales in March 1913, and later appeared against the Welsh for a second time and also starred in two internationals against Scotland, striking the winning goal in a 1–0 victory at Chelsea in April 1914. He also played for the Football League side three times and in the annual challenge match for Birmingham against London in 1909, 1911 and 1913. During the war, when he was badly gassed, he played as a guest for several top clubs, having one outing for Blues in December 1916.

Recruited by Blues to bolster their attack, Hampton – playing alongside Jack Whitehouse and record-signing Joe Lane in the forward line – scored 11 goals in his first 10 League games, nine coming in his first five, including a four-timer in an 8–0 home win over Nottingham Forest. He also netted twice on his debut in an emphatic 5–0 win at Barnsley.

Unfortunately Blues missed out on promotion, finishing third, but the following season, after Scotsman Johnny Crosbie was brought into the attack, Hampton maintained his form by firing in 16 goals in 34 games, helping Blues win the Second Division Championship. He bagged a treble against Leicester (won 5–0) and hit doubles in wins over Wolves (4–1), Stoke (2–1), Coventry City (4–0) and West Ham United (2–1). In 1921–22, when he was used as a right-half for a few games, he managed only four goals, Blues having introduced Joe Bradford and Jack Elkes in their attack as they attempted to establish themselves in the top flight.

Not getting any younger but still alert, Hampton moved to Newport County in September 1922 after scoring 31 goals in 59 first-class matches for Blues. He returned to Wellington Town in January 1924 and was later appointed coach at Preston North End (June 1925 to January 1926). He had two years playing Birmingham Works football and assisted non-League side Lilleshall Town before taking over as coach of Birmingham's Colts side (October 1934 to May 1937). He later ran the Carlton café in Queen Street, Rhyl, and in the summer season he was visited by scores of Villa and Birmingham supporters! He remained in North Wales and was almost 78 when he died in 1963.

Fred Harris

Date of birth: 2 July 1912, Solihull, Warwickshire
Died: 13 October 1998, South Warwickshire

Blues record:
Appearances: League 280, FA Cup 30, Wartime 94
Goals: League 61, FA Cup 8, Wartime 7
Debut: League, 25 August 1934 v Aston Villa (h) 2–1

Also played for: Sparkbrook FC, Birmingham Transport, Osborne Athletic

Fred Harris was associated with Birmingham City Football Club for a little over 17 years, appearing in first-team action before, during and after World War Two. After competing in local works football for many years, and doing very well, he was 20 years of age by the time he joined Blues as a full-time professional in March 1933. When he made a scoring League debut in a 2–1 win in the second city derby against rivals Aston Villa in front of 54,000 fans at St Andrew's in August 1934, he was occupying the inside-right position. After that impressive display, he comfortably held his place in the first team and netted 12 times in total that season (in 34 senior appearances) as Blues just managed to edge clear of the relegation zone after losing only one of their last six League games to finish 19th in the table, three points from disaster!

The following season Harris started out as Fred White's right-wing partner in the Blues attack, but was switched to inside-left to accommodate Tom Grosvenor after seven games. He went on to have another fine campaign, scoring 18 goals in 44 League and FA Cup matches.

In 1936–37 Harris and his new wing partner Seymour Morris were quite outstanding down Birmingham's left flank, and both players scored well, Morris netting 15 times to Fred's 11 – but their efforts didn't bring any reward as Blues hung around mid-table, never really threatening to rise much higher, but away from the relegation dog fight. Unfortunately he was injured towards the end of that season and was absent from the side until the 19th match of 1937–38, returning at a time when Blues were once more battling hard to pull clear of the relegation zone. He got stuck in, scored seven goals, six of them proving vital, and helped the side retain their First Division status.

In the last season prior to World War Two Harris top scored with 17 goals and played in the fifth-round FA Cup tie against Everton when a record crowd of 67,341 packed into St Andrew's to witness the 2–2 draw with the subsequent League champions. During the hostilities he scored seven goals in almost 100 regional League and Cup appearances for Blues, helping them win the Football League South title in 1945–46 ahead of Aston Villa on goal average. He had by now been switched to the right-half position, where he remained until announcing his retirement in May 1950, at the age of 38.

Harris skippered the first team on several occasions and gained a Second Division Championship medal in 1947–48 when he missed only two League games, playing in 36 the following year and 12 in 1949–50 when Blues were unfortunately relegated.

A honest-to-goodness performer, never flashy, always grafting hard and long, Harris made over 400 first-team appearances for Blues, with 310 coming at senior level. He also scored 76 goals and is listed in the top 20 of Birmingham's all-time appearance makers, and is one of only seven players who have starred in 30 or more FA Cup matches for the club. He also represented the Football League against the Scottish League at Ibrox Park in March 1949 and was twice named as reserve by England.

Harris qualified as a masseur and physiotherapist during the latter years of his playing career, and after hanging up his boots he ran his own chiropody business on Warwick Road, Olton, for many years. He was 86 when he died.

Bob Hatton

Date of birth: 10 April 1947, Hull

Blues record:
Appearances: League 170+5, FA Cup 15+1, League Cup 12, others 15
Goals: League 58, FA Cup 6, League Cup 5, others 4
Debut: League, 30 October 1971 v Burnley (a) drew 1–1

Also played for: Wath Wanderers, Bolton Wanderers, Northampton Town, Carlisle United, Blackpool, Luton Town, Sheffield United, Cardiff City, Lodge Cotterill FC

Nomadic striker Bob Hatton – referred to in some spent quarters as 'have boots will travel' – spent almost 19 years playing senior professional football (November 1964 to May 1983), and during that time he netted 217 goals in 620 League appearances, giving him a seasonal average of almost 11 goals in 31 games. His self analysis of 'give me three chances and I'll score from one' certainly rang true throughout his career.

Owing to the presence of John Richards, Derek Dougan, Peter Knowles and others, Hatton failed to have an impact with Wolves, netting eight goals in 13 outings. He spent 18 months with Bolton Wanderers from March 1967 to October 1968 where he played alongside his namesake Dave Hatton, scoring two goals in 24 appearances. He served Northampton Town until July 1969, claiming eight goals in 36 matches, and was registered with Carlisle United for just over two years, notching 40 goals in just over 100 senior games, before joining Blues in October 1971, signed by manager Freddie Goodwin.

Well-built with a neat touch, Hatton was strong in the air and could use both feet when shooting at goal, which he did at every given opportunity. He preferred to play in the inside-left position, from where he could either venture out wide or cut inside and dart through the middle. A tremendous all-round player, very skilful, he was a constant threat to opposing defences and proved to be the final cog in Blues' 1971–72 promotion-winning team, lining up in a forward line that also featured future England internationals Trevor Francis and Bob Latchford and left-winger Gordon Taylor. Between them, Francis, Hatton and Latchford scored 50 League goals that season and followed up in 1972–73 with another 32, adding 30 more to their total during the next 12 months before the strike force was broken up when Latchford moved to Everton.

Hatton was joined up front by Scotsman Kenny Burns for the 1974–75 campaign, and they performed exceedingly well together, helping Blues reach the FA Cup semi-finals, where they lost to Fulham in a replay. In fact, Hatton and, the more aggressive of the two, Burns struck home 26 goals in major competitions in their first season as partners, but in 1975–76 Hatton contributed just nine while his new colleague up front, another ex-Wolves player Peter Withe, also scored nine times, but the in-form Francis weighed in with 18.

A great favourite with the St Andrew's supporters, Hatton played well with each of his fellow strikers and his record for Blues (in first-class competitions) was exceptionally good – 73 goals in 218 appearances – an average of one goal every three games. He left St Andrew's in July 1976, when manager Willie Bell elected to go with just two main strikers up front. Immediately joining forces with Luton Town, he stayed at Kenilworth Road for two years, grabbing over 30 goals in 90 games before signing for Sheffield United, for whom he hit 43 goals in 118 matches. Subsequently ending his League career with Cardiff City after one season at Ninian Park (1982–83), when he struck nine goals in 29 starts, Hatton returned to non-League action later when assisting the strong Birmingham Sunday team Lodge Cotterill, kicking his last ball in earnest at the age of 40.

Nowadays Hatton, who still attends Blues' home matches quite regularly, is living in semi-retirement, having worked in the insurance industry for many years as well as acting as a match summariser on local radio. Still remarkably fit, he goes to his nearby gymnasium four or five times a week, where he does a lot of swimming and general exercise.

Mike Hellawell

Date of birth: 30 June 1938, Keighley, Yorkshire

Blues record:
Appearances: League 178, FA Cup 8, League Cup 16, Europe 11
Goals: League 30, FA Cup 0, League Cup 1, Europe 2
Debut: League, 7 September 1957 v Newcastle United (home) lost 4–1

Also played for: Salts FC, Huddersfield Town (two spells), Queen's Park Rangers, Sunderland, Peterborough United, Bromsgrove Rovers, England (2 full caps)

A fast-raiding outside-right who loved to hug the touchline, the red-haired Mike Hellawell was quick over distances of 25–30 yards. Exchanged for inside-forward Bill Finney, he moved to Birmingham City from Queen's Park Rangers in May 1957, recruited by manager Arthur Turner, initially as a replacement for Gordon Astall, having made less than 50 League appearances for the London club during his two years as a professional.

A Yorkshireman, born deep in the heart of Rugby League territory in Keighley, from where Trevor Hockey originated, Hellawell failed to make the grade with his first club Huddersfield Town, but he did much better with Queen's Park Rangers, missing only two League games in 1956–57 (scoring seven goals). Having represented the Third Division South against the North in the annual challenge match, a number of First Division clubs began to take a interest in the flying winger, including Arsenal and Sunderland, but it was Blues who swooped first, enticing him to the Midlands a month before his 19th birthday. He scored on his Blues debut in September 1957 versus Newcastle United, when he deputised for England international Astall, but spent his first two seasons at St Andrew's playing reserve-team football. In fact, he made only two senior appearances in that time, and then, when fellow winger Harry Hooper was secured from Wolverhampton Wanderers, his future with Blues looked in doubt. However, he stuck to his task and in 1959–60 played in 11 League matches as well as in the semi-final of the Inter Cities Fairs Cup.

Hellawell became more of a regular in 1960–61 when he appeared in the Fairs Cup Final defeat by AS Roma and scored Blues' first League Cup goal in their initial tie against Bradford Park Avenue (away) at the end of October. An ever present the following season when he netted seven goals in 46 League and Cup games, he and Jimmy Bloomfield formed a superb right-wing partnership, and the press suggested at one stage that the two players wouldn't let England down if chosen together.

Hellawell continued to perform exceedingly well in 1962–63, scoring five times in 51 outings. He gained a League Cup-winners' tankard, when Blues beat neighbours Aston Villa in the two-leg Final, and was outstanding in the first game at St Andrew's, giving Villa's normally sound left-back Charlie Aitken a torrid time in a 3–1 win. He was kept quiet in the return fixture, which ended goalless. He also won two full England caps, both in October 1962 when he lined up in place of Blackburn's Bryan Douglas against France in a European Championship qualifier at Hillsborough (drew 1–1) and Northern Ireland in Belfast (won 3–1).

After losing his form and subsequently his place in the Blues side, replaced by the former West Bromwich Albion forward Alec Jackson, Hellawell moved north to Sunderland in January 1965. He remained at Roker Park for 20 months, making 46 appearances. He returned to Huddersfield in September 1966 and added 54 games to his tally before rounding off his League career with a spell at Peterborough United, having nine outings from December 1968. He served with non-League side Bromsgrove Rovers from August 1969 until May 1971 when he announced his retirement from football. After hanging up his boots, he ran a shop for many years in his native Keighley.

Besides being a fine footballer, Hellawell was also a talented all-round cricketer. He played for several minor clubs, including Walsall (Birmingham League), Keighley and Crossflatts CC, and represented Warwickshire against Oxford University at Edgbaston in 1962, when, as a middle-order, right-hand batsman, he scored 29 and 30 not out and as a bowler took four wickets for 54 runs.

Terry Hennessey

Date of birth: 1 September 1942, Llay near Wrexham

Blues record:

Appearances: League 178, FA Cup 6, League Cup 12, Europe 6
Goals: League 3, FA Cup 0, League Cup 0, Europe 0
Debut: League, 22 March 1961 v Manchester City (h) won 3–2

Also played for: Nottingham Forest, Derby County, Tulsa Roughnecks, Vancouver Whitecaps, Wales (six Under-23 and 39 full caps)
Managed: Tamworth, Tulsa Roughnecks, Shepshed Charterhouse, Kimberley Town, Heildelberg (Australia)

Terry Hennessey represented Wrexham & District Boys and was capped by Wales at Schoolboy level as an inside-forward before joining Birmingham City as a junior in June 1958, turning professional in September 1959. He began his senior career as an attacking wing-half, but was later, perhaps controversially in some people's minds, switched to a defensive position where, for most of the time, he performed as a sweeper. In fact, during the early 1960s he was rated by many as one of the best defenders in the game, producing some excellent performances, especially for Blues, whom he skippered on several occasions.

With only seven League games under his belt, Hennessey turned out to be the star player when Blues beat Inter Milan in the semi-final of the 1961 Fairs Cup, and he did very well in the Final against AS Roma, which Blues lost over two legs. Two years later he was again instrumental when Blues defeated arch-rivals Aston Villa to win the League Cup, also on aggregate – their first major trophy in the club's history.

Strong, athletic and a fine passer of the ball, Hennessey went on appear in more than 200 first-class games for Blues, being an inspirational battler in several relegation campaigns before transferring to Nottingham Forest for a giveaway price of just £45,000 in November 1965, six months after Blues had been demoted to the Second Division. He established himself as a regular in the Blues side in 1961–62 and was an ever present the following season when he scored his first senior goal – a decisive one in a 3–2 win over West Ham United when Blues were fighting for the lives at the wrong end of the Division One table. He missed only seven League games during the next two campaigns before moving to the City Ground just four months into the 1965–66 season.

Hennessey, who looked older than he was due to his receding hairline, replaced Jeff Whitefoot in the Nottingham Forest middle line. He became the driving force in midfield, carrying the ball out of defence in style to coax on his forwards. He was captain of Forest in 1966–67 when they finished runners-up in the First Division and reached the FA Cup semi-final.

In February 1970, after adding 183 senior appearances to his career tally and undergoing an operation for appendicitis, Hennessey was one of a handful of players transferred by Forest manager Matt Gillies. Surprisingly, he joined East Midlands neighbours Derby County, becoming the Rams' first six-figure signing at £110,000. In 1972, under Brian Clough's management, he gained both League Championship and Texaco Cup-winners' medals with the Rams, and before leaving the Baseball Ground he took his tally of full international caps with Wales up to 39 – having gained his first against Northern Ireland in April 1962 when the Irish were thumped 4–0 in Cardiff, Terry helping set up two of John Charles's four goals. Earlier, he had represented his country in six Under-23 internationals, all as a Blues player.

In April 1974, having had two cartilage operations, Hennessey pulled out of competitive football to take over as manager of non-League side Tamworth. Three years later he took charge of Kimberley Town and then had a spell in the NASL as assistant-coach of Tulsa Roughnecks before returning to England in 1978 as coach to Shepshed Charterhouse, holding office for two years. There followed a second spell with the Roughnecks, initially as a coach in 1980 then as chief coach-manager from 1981 to 1983, and his next appointment took him to Vancouver Whitecaps as assistant manager-coach to the former Wolves, Forest and Derby winger Alan Hinton. Terry then held a coaching position in Toronto before having a season as boss of the Australian club Heidelberg in Victoria State in 1987–88.

Jim Herriot

Date of birth: 20 December 1939, Chapelhall near Airdrie, Lanarkshire

Blues record:

Appearances: League 181, FA Cup 20, League Cup 11
Goals: 0
Debut: League, 21 August 1965 v Crystal Palace (h) won 2–1

Also played for: Douglasdale Juniors, Dunfermline Athletic (two spells), Aston Villa, Mansfield Town, Durban City, Hibernian, St Mirren, Partick Thistle, Greenock Morton (two spells), Scotland (2 B and 8 full caps)

Goalkeeper Jim Herriot plied his trade with non-League side Douglasdale Juniors before gaining a Scottish Cup runners'-up medal with Dunfermline Athletic in April 1965. The following month he joined Blues and became a big favourite with the St Andrew's fans. Known as the 'Clown Prince', he often daubed boot polish, American-football style, under his eyes to divert the glare of the floodlights during evening matches and even rubbed dirt on his face to divert the glare of the sun... even if the sun wasn't shining! He remembered 'My manager at Dunfermline Jock Stein gave me the idea of using polish as war paint, and I rarely started a game without two black eyes!

'Everyone thought I'd been involved in a punch up. I did it because I hated wearing a cap, and sometimes on a sunny day I used to rub dirt into my face.'

An infuriating 'keeper at times, brilliant one minute, scary the next, Herriot could produce a stunning save and then let in a silly goal from a weaker effort or drop the ball from a high, looping centre, which invariably resulted in a goal being scored against his side. Some supporters and, indeed, his teammates, even nicknamed him 'Dracula', simply because he hated crosses, but that apart, he was a fine 'keeper who went on to appear in well over 200 first-class matches for Blues after replacing Johnny Schofield between the posts at the start of the 1965–66 Second Division season following relegation at the end of the previous term. He played in both the 1967 League Cup and 1968 FA Cup semi-finals for Blues and was an ever present in 1966–67 (55 games). He missed only two League matches out of a possible 148 between November 1965 and April 1969.

Herriot was eventually replaced by Mike Kelly, and on leaving St Andrew's in August 1971, following loan spells during the previous season with second city rivals Aston Villa, Third Division outfit Mansfield Town and one of South Africa's best-known clubs Durban City, he returned to his home country to sign for Hibernian. At the end of his first season at Easter Road, he collected a second Scottish Cup runners'-up prize (after Hibs had crashed 6–1 to Celtic), but he made up for that disappointment 12 months later when he helped the Edinburgh club win the Scottish League Cup and also the pre-season Dryburgh Cup.

In February 1975 Herriot was transferred to Partick Thistle, and after a loan spell with Greenock Morton he returned to his former club Dunfermline Athletic in 1976 before ending his playing career back at Morton, officially retiring in the summer of 1977, although, in his own words, he thought he could have gone on for at least another 'couple of years'.

Capped eight times by Scotland at senior level, Herriot's first international appearance was against Denmark in Copenhagen in October 1968 (won 1–0) and his last came 12 months later against West Germany in Hamburg (won 3–1). He also played twice against Cyprus, the Scots winning 5–0 in Nicosia and 8–0 in Glasgow. As well as his exploits with Scotland's senior team, he served his country at both B and Under-23 levels and twice represented the Scottish League as a Dunfermline player, and today he enjoys ever-lasting fame following the adoption of his surname by the famous veterinarian author and ardent Birmingham City supporter Alf Wright, whose pseudonym was, of course, James Herriot. Alf Wright died in 1995, but goalkeeper Herriot continued to work as a bricklayer in Larkhall well into his 60s, and today he remains very much a keen football supporter, following the fortunes of Birmingham City with interest.

Terry Hibbitt

Date of birth:	1 February 1947, Bradford, Yorkshire
Died:	5 August 1994, Ponteland near Newcastle-upon-Tyne

Blues record:

Appearances:	League 110, FA Cup 5, League Cup 4, others 3
Goals:	League 11, FA Cup 0, League Cup 0, others 0
Debut:	League, 6 September 1975 v Queen's Park Rangers (h) drew 1–1

Also played for: Leeds United, Newcastle United (two spells), Gateshead

Midfielder Terry Hibbitt had three excellent seasons with Birmingham City. Enthusiastic, energetic and competitive, at 5ft 7ins tall he became a firm favourite with the St Andrew's faithful, who were bitterly disappointed when he left the club to return to Newcastle in May 1978. Brother of Kenny Hibbitt, who played for Bradford Park Avenue, Wolverhampton Wanderers, Coventry City and Bristol Rovers and also managed Cardiff City and Walsall, he was an apprentice at Elland Road before being upgraded to the professional ranks by Leeds United manager Don Revie in December 1964.

Although regarded as a reserve to the likes of Billy Bremner, Johnny Giles and Bobby Collins, Hibbitt nevertheless shared in some of Leeds' glories, playing in the 1968 Inter Cities Fairs Cup Final and helping them finish runners-up in the First Division in 1966 and win the Championship three years later, making 12 appearances.

In August 1971 Hibbitt was transferred to Newcastle United for £30,000 – being regarded as one of the club's finest-ever signings – and three years later played in the FA Cup Final defeat by Liverpool at Wembley. Unfortunately he was injured soon afterwards and at one point his career was in jeopardy. He missed several games but recovered his fitness and went on to make a total of 160 appearances for the Geordies (eight goals scored) before moving to Birmingham City in a £100,000 deal in August 1975, recruited by manager Freddie Goodwin.

Playing alongside Howard Kendall and Alan Campbell in the Blues midfield, Hibbitt produced some outstanding performances, and after Campbell had departed he shouldered most of the responsibilities in the engine room until the arrival of Tony Towers and Gary Emmanuel, who established themselves in the side in 1977–78.

Hibbitt was a wonderful passer of the ball, often driving it across field up to 40 yards. He could also shoot and created opportunities galore for his strikers. He netted three times in his first season with Blues, who escaped relegation from the top flight by the skin of their teeth after winning two and drawing one of their last four games. The following season he was an ever present and had the pleasure of scoring in a 2–1 derby win over Aston Villa. In his last season at St Andrew's he missed one game (at QPR) and netted six times, including two in a 3–1 victory over Derby County and one, to no avail, in a thrilling 5–4 home defeat by Chelsea.

On his return to St James' Park in a transaction that brought winger Stewart Barrowclough to St Andrew's, Hibbitt was immediately made captain of Newcastle, taking his appearance tally up to 259 before a knee injury ended his senior career in the summer of 1981, although he still turned out for Gateshead, helping them win the Northern Premier title, and represented the FA's non-League side. Later appointed player-coach of the north-east club, he took over as team manager in April 1986 before moving in the same capacity to Durham City (October 1986 to April 1987). He accumulated a total of 434 senior appearances for his three major League clubs, scoring 33 goals while creating many more.

After leaving football Hibbitt ran a newsagents in Newcastle and also worked as a milkman for a short time before settling down as manager of a pub in Ponteland on the outskirts of his adopted home of Newcastle.

Terry died from cancer at the age of 46.

Harry Hibbs

Date of birth: 27 May 1906, Wilnecote near Tamworth, Staffs
Died: 23 May 1984, Hatfield, Hertfordshire

Blues record:
Appearances: League 358, FA Cup 30, Wartime 12
Goals: 0
Debut: League, 1 May 1926 v Arsenal (a) lost 3–0

Also played for: Wilnecote Holy Trinity FC, Tamworth Castle, de Havillands FC, England (25 full caps)
Managed: Walsall, Ware Town, Welwyn Garden City

For almost a decade between 1929 and 1938, Harry Hibbs was regarded as one of the finest goalkeepers in the Football League and during that time he won 25 full caps for England, gaining both his first and last against Wales, in November 1929 and February 1936. He was on the losing side only five times and conceded 26 goals. He also played in three international trials, represented the Football League against the Scottish League on three occasions (1929–33) and toured South Africa and Canada with the FA party in 1929 and 1931 respectively, gaining one extra cap each time.

Born into a goalkeeping family – his uncle Hubert Pearson and his cousin Harold, Hubert's son, both served with West Bromwich Albion, while another cousin, Horace Pearson, assisted Coventry City – Hibbs started out as an inside-forward and after switching to keeping goal he was spotted playing for his local club Tamworth Castle. He joined Blues as an amateur in May 1924 and turned professional a month later, making his League debut on the last day of the 1925–26 season at Highbury against the First Division runners-up Arsenal, when he deputised for Dan Tremelling.

Playing only occasionally – making just 32 senior appearances in four seasons – Hibbs eventually took over the number-one position from Tremelling in 1929 and remained first choice between the posts for Blues until Frank Clack came on to the scene during the 1938–39 campaign.

Extraordinary for his gift of anticipation, which enabled him to get his body behind the ball when saving the hardest shot, he was both daring and agile, and, although on the small side, relatively lightweight and pale-faced, he was pretty useful in the air and on the ground, often choosing to punch the ball rather than catch it when challenged by a tough centre-forward. Totally unflappable, he missed only nine League games in 1929–30 and six the following season when Blues reached the FA Cup Final, where they lost 2–1 to Midlands neighbours West Bromwich Albion, Harry lining up opposite his cousin Harold Pearson. In fact, he took over from Harry, who was not quite match fit, after a spell on the injured list, for the home international match against Scotland at Wembley in April 1932.

In the 1931–32 campaign Hibbs was brilliant at times, producing immaculate displays against the League champions-elect Everton at St Andrew's, when Blues won 4–0, and in two other home matches against Middlesbrough (won 3–0) and Leicester City (won 2–0). In 1932–33 he was absent twice before having his worst season in terms of appearances since gaining his place in the side in 1933–34 (31 starts). The following season he was again in tip-top form as Blues were forced to work overtime to retain their top-flight status, and thereafter Harry, who took over as captain, maintained his form as Blues again found themselves fighting for points at the wrong end of the table. Older supporters said that if it hadn't been for Harry then Blues would have been relegated long before they were – in 1939 after he had virtually decided to retire.

Hibbs eventually took off his green jersey in May 1940 after having a testimonial match at St Andrew's against Aston Villa. His record of 388 senior appearances is the third-highest ever made by a Blues goalkeeper, behind Tremelling's total of 395 and Gil Merrick's tally of 551. He was manager of Walsall from August 1944 to June 1951 and remained in football until 1964 when he retired to live in Welwyn Garden City. Harry attended his last Blues match in 1972 as a guest at St Andrew's.

Trevor Hockey

Date of birth:	1 May 1943, Keighley, Yorkshire
Died:	2 April 1987, Keighley, Yorkshire

Blues record:

Appearances:	League 195+1, FA Cup 19, League Cup 16
Goals:	League 8, FA Cup 1, League Cup 4
Debut:	League, 20 November 1975 v Coventry City (h) lost 1–0
Also played for:	Keighley Central Youth Club, Bradford City (two spells), Nottingham Forest, Newcastle United, Sheffield United, Norwich City, Aston Villa, Athlone Town (player-manager), San Diego Jaws (NASL), San Jose Earthquakes (NASL), Las Vegas Quicksilver (NASL), Wales (9 full caps)
Managed:	Stalybridge Celtic

Trevor Hockey was a very colourful character and one of the fiercest competitors in the game. Having played two codes of rugby, Union for Abertillery and League for Keighley, he chose the round ball game, and after a spell as an orthodox inside-forward he switched to the wing, preferring the right to the left, and later played in midfield where his strong, aggressive style made him into a splendid ball winner. His great determination and sometimes over zealous tackling often brought him into conflict with referees, and, in fact, he was sent off in his last international for Wales against Poland in Katowice in 1974.

Always giving 100 percent out on the field and nothing less, Hockey's natural driving spirit inspired those around him, and he went on to make well over 600 appearances in club and international football in a career that spanned almost 20 years. In fact, it is believed that Trevor became the first player to appear in a first-class game on all 92 League grounds that were being used when he was in his prime.

During his school days Hockey represented West Riding Under-19s and was playing for a local youth-club team when he joined Bradford City as an amateur in June 1958, turning professional in May 1960. He moved to Nottingham Forest for £15,000 in November 1961 and two years later signed for Newcastle United for a fee of £25,000, arriving at St Andrew's in November 1965, Blues manager Stan Cullis paying £22,500 for his services. He took over from Alec Jackson as Blues' outside-right before moving to the opposite flank later in the season. In 1966–67 he again occupied both wing positions and also lined up at inside-right as Blues reached the semi-finals of the League Cup and the quarter-finals of the FA Cup.

In 1967–68, with Blues fighting hard to keep in touch with the clubs challenging for promotion from the Second Division, Hockey was instrumental in helping the team reach the FA Cup semi-finals, beaten 2–0 by West Bromwich Albion. During the late 1960s and early 1970s he manned the Blues midfield very efficiently along with the likes of Johnny Vincent, Ron Wylie, Albert Murray, Alan Campbell and others, producing at times some brilliant displays. So much so that in January 1971 he was approached by and eventually sold to Sheffield United for £35,000, having made over 230 first-class appearances for Blues.

Hockey helped the Blades gain promotion to the top flight in his first half a season at Bramall Lane and after that became a soccer nomad, assisting, in turn, Norwich City, whom he helped save from relegation, Aston Villa, Bradford City (again), the Irish club Athlone Town and three different clubs in the North American Soccer League. He later managed Stalybridge Celtic in 1977–78 and ran soccer coaching classes at a holiday camp before attempting to introduce football to Keighley Rugby Club.

On the international front, Hockey won nine full caps for Wales, starting off in 1972 against Finland when he became the first 'Anglo' to represent the Principality at senior level, qualifying through his father, also a former Rugby League player with Keighley, who was born in Abertillery.

In the latter stages of his playing career Hockey grew long hair and a thick, black beard, making him readily recognisable on the field and earning him the nickname of 'Dai Fungus'. He was approaching his 44th birthday when he sadly died, still in his kit, after playing in a five-a-side match at Keighley.

Billy Hughes

Date of birth: 6 March 1918, Carmarthen
Died: 16 June 1981, Birmingham

Blues record:
Appearances: League 104, FA Cup 6, Wartime 55
Goals: 0
Debut: League, 25 January 1936 v Manchester City (h) lost 1–0

Also played for: Archer Corinthians, Llanelli, Watcher's Celtic FC, Llanelli Town, Swansea Town (loan), World War Two guest for Arsenal, Chester, Heart of Midlothian, Queen's Park Rangers, Tottenham Hotspur and West Ham United, Luton Town, Chelsea, Hereford United, Flint Town United, Wales (10 full, 14 wartime caps), Great Britain (1 cap)

A former Swansea Grammar school pupil and Llanelli Boys representative player, Billy Hughes – who was employed as an apprentice car mechanic – had a brief flirtation playing Rugby Union before taking up soccer seriously with the Llanelli-based non-League side Archer Corinthians. He assisted a handful of other local teams and had a loan spell with Swansea Town to gain experience.

Hughes certainly made rapid progress, and in May 1935 Birmingham signed him as a professional, handing him his League debut as a 17-year-old against Manchester City at St Andrew's in mid-January 1936, when he deputised at left-back for the injured Billy Steel. The following year he became a regular in the side and, with Cyril Trigg, set up a Football League record for the youngest-ever pair of full-backs when they faced Preston North End in a First Division game on 27 March 1937.

Hughes took over the Blues captaincy from goalkeeper Harry Hibbs in 1938, and during that relegation season (1938–39) he played his first full international for Wales against Scotland, later adding a further nine to his collection, as well as gaining 14 Wartime caps, the second highest number behind his clubmate Don Dearson.

During the hostilities Hughes – who guested for several top-class sides up and down the country – was switched successfully into the centre-half position and was re-appointed skipper of the team, helping Blues win the Football League South Championship in 1946 on goal average from their near neighbours Aston Villa. When peacetime football returned in the mid–1940s, he reverted back to his former, and favourite, position of full-back, and at one stage he was regarded as the best left-back in the country, having the honour of representing Great Britain against the Rest of Europe in front of 135,000 fans at Hampden Park in 1947.

In July 1947 Hughes was transferred to Luton Town for a record fee of £11,000, and although great things were expected of him his stay at Kenilworth Road was a brief one as he switched his allegiance to Chelsea in March 1948, signed for £15,000.

A polished and skilful defender, Hughes quit competitive League football in the summer of 1951, joining Hereford United, who were then members of the old Southern League. He moved to Flint Town United of the Welsh League North in January 1954 and retired the following summer at the age of 37, soon after captaining the underdogs to a sensational Welsh Cup Final victory over Chester, having knocked out Cardiff City in the semi-final. He went on to become licensee of the Bluebell Inn at Halkyn while also scouting for Chester. He returned to the West Midlands in 1969 to become steward of the Wolesley Car Social club. He was aged 63 when he died in 1981.

Roger Hynd

Date of birth: 2 February 1942, Falkirk, Scotland

Blues record:
Appearances: League 162+8, FA Cup 11, League Cup 17, others 8
Goals: League 4, FA Cup 1, League Cup 0, others 0
Debut: League, 15 August 1970 v Queen's Park Rangers (h) won 2–1

Also played for: Glasgow Rangers, Crystal Palace, Oxford United, Walsall
Managed: Motherwell

Nephew of the great Bill Shankly, Roger Shankly Hynd was a well-built defender, as solid as a rock, who possessed the physique of a weight-lifter and was rarely, if ever, muscled off the ball. Strong both in the air and on the ground, he had a distinctive running style, which involved a very high knee lift, signalling him out above the rest of the team, and he despised finishing second best at anything. He became a great favourite with the fans and gave Blues excellent service for five years, during which time he accumulated over 200 first-team appearances and helped the team gain promotion to the First Division in 1972.

Prior to moving to St Andrew's for £25,000 in July 1970, Hynd had made 38 appearances for Crystal Palace, having earlier netted five goals in 48 senior outings for Rangers, gaining a European Cup-winners' Cup runners'-up medal in 1967 when the Scottish club lost 1–0 to the German side Bayern Munich in the Final in Nuremburg. He had signed professional forms at Ibrox Park at the age of 17 and made his debut in Scottish League football during the 1963–64 season when the Gers won the League Championship for the second season running. In fact, he was named as a reserve for three domestic Cup Finals during his time with the Glasgow club.

Signed by manager Freddie Goodwin, Hynd, who was nicknamed 'Garth', although his teammates referred to him as 'Pele' for a while after one bewildering series of dummies in his own six-yard box, immediately took over at centre-half in the Blues defence, Dave Robinson switching to the left-half berth to accompany him. He made an impressive debut against Queen's Park Rangers and missed only two League games during his first season at St Andrew's as Blues finished ninth in the Second Division.

During the next campaign Stan Harland was brought in to partner him at the heart of the Blues defence, the duo proving to be a combination of skill, muscle and brains, and they were superb together, helping the team claim second place in the table and so regain their First Division status after a break of seven years, Hynd being an ever present and scoring his first goals for the club in a 3–0 third-round FA Cup win over Port Vale and in the 4–0 home League victory over Norwich City seven weeks later.

After the first three months of the 1972–73 season, Hynd found himself with a new defensive partner, John Roberts, ex-Arsenal, taking over from Harland, and they quickly drew up a fine understanding, Roger producing some excellent displays as Blues consolidated themselves in the top flight. The following season manager Goodwin used Roberts, Kenny Burns and Joe Gallagher alongside him in the Blues back four, but this time things were much harder in the League as Blues had to battle to stay clear of the relegation zone, staying up in 19th position.

Unfortunately injuries began to affect Hynd's game in 1974–75, and he started only eight senior games, missing out on Blues' run to the FA Cup semi-finals where they lost to Fulham after a replay. With Gallagher and Garry Pendrey now bedded into the two central-defensive positions with others in reserve, he became surplus to requirements, and after a loan spell with Oxford United (October–November 1975) new manager Willie Bell transferred him to nearby Walsall (December 1975). He remained at Fellows Park for three years before returning to Scotland to become manager of Motherwell, later taking employment as a physical training instructor in Wishaw, having qualified as such some years earlier.

Probably the only Blues player ever to play a trombone, Hynd now lives in retirement in his native Scotland, but he has suffered with his health of late.

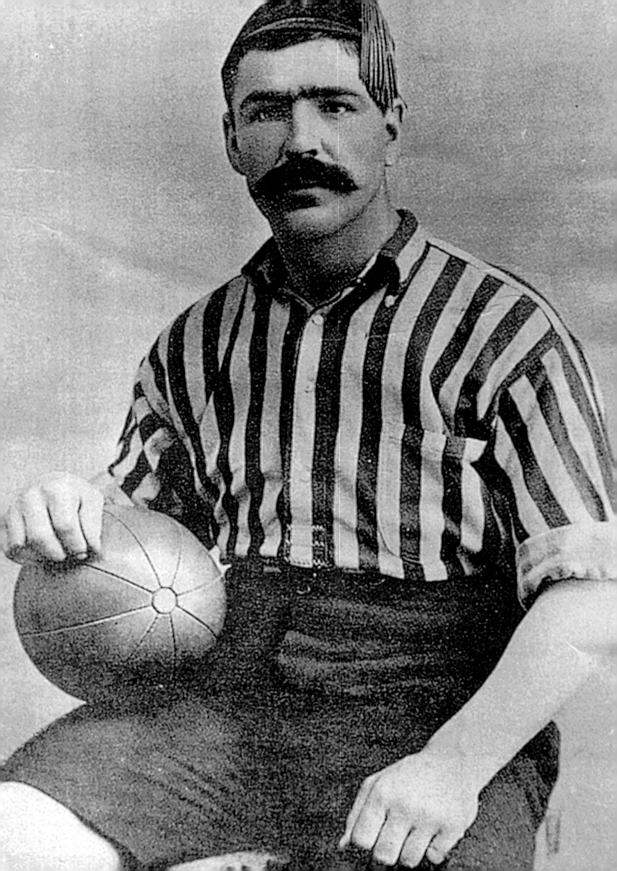

Caeser Jenkyns

Date of birth: 24 August 1866, Builth, South Wales
Died: 23 July 1941, Birmingham

Blues record:
Appearances: League 75, FA Cup 21, Test Matches 3
Goals: League 11, FA Cup 2, Test Matches 0
Debut: FA Cup, 27 October 1888 v Burslem Port Vale (h) won 3–2

Also played for: Small Heath St Andrew's, Walsall Swifts, Unity Gas Works (two spells), Woolwich Arsenal, Newton Heath (now Manchester United), Walsall (two spells), Coventry City, Saltney Wednesday, Birmingham City Police Force, Wales (8 full caps)

A big, burly defender, Caesar Augustus Llewelyn Jenkyns was a player of no little skill and a master of the shoulder charge. He was reputed to have a fearsome but fair charge and woe betide any opponent who thought they could get the better of him in a 50–50 challenge. One reporter described him as having 'an atomic shoulder charge' and it is said that he once sent an opposing forward flying 20 yards across the field into the perimeter fence. Oh yes, he was a tough character alright and many forwards carried the legacy of several bruises after facing the Welshman.

Jenkyns had a heart as big as his huge 14st frame and was a source of great inspiration to his teammates. He regularly marched out onto the pitch before the start of a game with his sleeves rolled up and clapping his hands. He was always up for a fight. He captained virtually every team he played for – simply because he was a born leader. His strong physique enabled him to get tremendous distance with his heading and kicking, and he once entered and won a competition for long-distance kicking, banging the ball downfield fully 100 yards, one bounce, from a dead position.

Unfortunately the physicality of his game got Jenkyns into trouble with officials on a number of occasions. He was a player (opponent) supporters loved to hate, and in one game at Derby in March 1895 he lost his cool by dashing into the crowd and attempting to assault two spectators! The Blues management committee decided to dispense with his services at that point and suspended him for the remainder of the season.

Jenkyns played for Blues (Small Heath) from July 1888 (signed from the Unity Gas club) until April 1895 when he joined Woolwich Arsenal. He made his senior debut in the second qualifying round of the FA Cup against Burslem Port Vale, scored his first goal in the next round against Leek (won 4–0) and then played in Blues' first-ever League game against Port Vale in September 1892, gaining a Second Division Championship-winners' medal that season when he missed only one match. The following season he was instrumental as Blues finished runners-up in the same Division and this time took their place in the top flight after beating Darwen in a Test Match. He played the first of his eight internationals for Wales in 1892 against Ireland, collecting his last six years later against England, by which time he had become a Walsall player.

Jenkyns spent a season with Arsenal (scoring six goals in 27 games) and 18 months with Newton Heath/Manchester United (netting six times in 47 starts). He spent five years with the Saddlers (claiming two goals in 88 appearances) and ended his senior career by having six outings with Coventry City in 1902–03. He later took over the George Inn at Moxley near Wednesbury before serving in the Birmingham City police force. His son, Octavius, had trials with Birmingham before World War One.

* A ceremony, unique in the annuls of Association football, took place at The Hawthorns, home of West Bromwich Albion, in 1934 when 68-year-old Jenkyns was presented with an international cap inscribed with the years covering his appearances for Wales. The Welsh FA did not present caps during his playing days, and when the player contacted Mr Ted Robbins, secretary of the association, pointing out that he had nothing to show for his international career, it was decided that a belated 'cap' should be awarded. Former England winger Billy Bassett handed the cap to him.

Dennis Jennings

Date of birth: 20 July 1910, Habberley Valley, Kidderminster
Died: 15 March 1996, Wadebridge, Cornwall

Blues record:
Appearances: League 192, FA Cup 22, Wartime 164
Goals: League 12, FA Cup 2, Wartime 3
Debut: League, 18 January 1936 v Manchester City (h) lost 1–0

Also played for: Franche FC (Kidderminster), St Barnabas FC, Foley Park, Stourport Swifts, Romsley Village, West Bromwich Albion (amateur), Kidderminster Harriers (two spells), Huddersfield Town, Grimsby Town, Nottingham Forest (guest), Lockheed Leamington.

Dennis Jennings occupied every position for Blues except centre-half, twice taking over in goal during a game when the regular 'keeper had gone off injured. An exceptionally good athlete, able to use both feet, he possessed a strong shot (mainly right-footed) and his speciality was his bicycle-kick, which he perfected late in his career after becoming a defender. Sometimes his flying leg got far too near the head of an opposing player for comfort!

A terrific club man, dedicated to playing football, Jennings remained a professional at St Andrew's for 15 years – from January 1936 until March 1951. He was the club's oldest player when he left at the age of 40 years and 10 months. During that time he appeared in 386 first-team matches, helping Blues win the Football League South Championship in 1946 and the Second Division title two seasons later when he made 29 appearances in one of the tightest defences in the game. Blues in fact conceded only 24 goals in 42 League games that season, 18 when Dennis was in the side.

Jennings started his footballing career as a utility forward with his local non-League side Franche, and after assisting several other intermediate clubs in the area he joined West Bromwich Albion as an amateur in 1928. Unfortunately he never made the breakthrough at The Hawthorns, and after a spell with Kidderminster Harriers he signed as a full-time professional for Huddersfield Town (October 1930). He scored five goals in 33 senior appearances for the Terriers and followed up by netting 29 times in 102 League and FA Cup games for Grimsby Town, for whom he served from September 1932 until his transfer to Blues for £1,200 halfway through the 1935–36 season.

Jennings, by now an established outside-right, went straight into the first team at St Andrew's and notched one goal (in a 4–2 home win over Blackburn Rovers) in 18 outings that season. In 1936–37 he occupied both the right and left-wing positions and also lined up at inside-right and then late in the following season he was switched into the half-back position, where he played on both flanks with Norman Brunskill in the middle. Back in the forward line for most of the 1938–39 campaign, he produced some useful performances in a struggling side as Blues slipped out of the First Division for the first time since 1921, and before he could get to grips with relegation World War Two started and competitive League and Cup football was suspended for its duration.

During the hostilities Jennings continued to play whenever possible, making 164 regional League and Cup appearances for Blues while also assisting Nottingham Forest as a guest in 1940–41. By the time peacetime football returned in 1945–46 he had been switched to left-back, a position he held until leaving Blues in 1951, when he returned to his former club Kidderminster Harriers as player-coach. He and Ken Green were exceptional together during the 1947–48 and 1948–49 seasons before injuries started to interrupt his game, so much so that Green was moved over into the left-back position, thus allowing the versatile Jack Badham to come into the side on the opposite flank.

Jennings continued playing football right through to 1955, serving Lockheed Leamington for two years after leaving Kidderminster. On his retirement at the age of 45, he moved 250 miles south to Cornwall where, for many years, he helped his brother run a caravan park at Little Dinham on the outskirts of Wadebridge. He visited St Andrew's whenever he could, right up until 1990, and he was 85 when he died.

Michael Johnson

Date of birth: 4 July 1973, Nottingham

Blues record:
Appearances: League 227+35, FA Cup 6+4, League Cup 25+6, others 11
Goals: League 13, FA Cup 0, League Cup 5, others 0
Debut: League, 2 September 1995 v Barnsley (a) won 5–0

Also played for: Clifton All Whites, Notts County, Derby County, Jamaica (14 full caps)

Defender Michael Johnson was one of Blues' unsung heroes. He spent eight seasons at St Andrew's, during which time he appeared in well over 300 competitive matches, scoring 18 goals.

Prior to joining Blues for £225,000 in September 1995, Johnson had represented Nottingham Schoolboys and also assisted his local club Clifton All Whites before signing for Notts County as an apprentice in July 1989, turning professional in July 1991, just after he had been voted Young Player of the Year. He went on to appear in 136 first-team matches for the Meadow Lane club, helping the Magpies win the Anglo-Italian Cup in 1995, having finished runners-up in the same competition 12 months earlier.

A catalogue of injuries gave Johnson his chance in the first team at Notts County. He made his senior debut against Sheffield United in a Zenith Data Systems Cup tie in October 1991 and four days later successfully marked hot-shot Ian Wright when the Magpies lost 2–0 to Arsenal at Highbury. He went on to produce some excellent displays over the next few years despite County suffering relegation to the Second Division.

Signed to bolster up the Blues' defence by manager Barry Fry, Johnson made an immediate impression on the St Andrew's faithful as a cultured central-defender. A solid tackler, strong in the air, he was also exceptionally quick over the ground and was rarely beaten for pace, especially when running 25–30 yards with an opponent. He acted as the perfect foil, first to co-defender Liam Daish and later to Gary Breen. Nicknamed 'Magic' after the famous American basketball player, he preferred to play on the left hand side of the defence, and in that initial season he made 43 appearances, following up with 39 in 1996–97 and 45 in 1997–98, when he also had the pleasure of scoring his first ever senior goal after 250 games, for Blues in the home League encounter against Sheffield United in the February (won 2–0).

A very adaptable player, able to occupy both full-back and the centre-half positions, Johnson was also blessed with two good feet and at times was also used as a man-marker by his new manager Trevor Francis, who described him in 1998 as one of the best centre-backs in the First Division. In 1998–99 he was named Blues' vice-captain to Martyn O'Connor after defender Gary Ablett was injured, and he seemed to thrive on the responsibility by scoring some vital goals, including a real cracker at Tranmere Rovers in March, which proved to be the winner (1–0), having netted twice in the 2–2 draw against the same opposition earlier in the season. Another goal earned a point at Huddersfield (1–1), and he was on target in a 4–2 home win over Bristol City in late November.

Johnson lost his place in the side halfway through the next campaign, after being away on international duty with Jamaica. Having made his debut against Sweden in May 1999, he then took part in the Guangzhou tournament in China and the CONCACEF Gold Cup Finals in the US (early in 2000) and at the end of season participated in the Hassan Cup in Morocco. He was a model of consistency during the 2000–01 season when Blues took the runners'-up prize in the League Cup Final, but then he feared for his future after Steve Bruce had taken over as boss, being left out of the team. However, he fought his way back into contention, produced some superb displays and helped the team gain promotion to the Premiership after a penalty shoot-out victory in the Play-off Final against Norwich City.

Johnson left Blues for Derby County in August 2003 and two years later helped the Rams reach the First Division Play-offs.

Billy Jones

Date of birth: 24 March 1881, Tipton, Staffordshire
Died: October 1948, Brighton, Sussex

Blues record:
Appearances: League 236, FA Cup 16
Goals: League 99, FA Cup 3
Debut: League, 19 October 1901 v Sheffield United (h) won 5–1

Also played for: Princes End (Tipton), Smethwick Town, Halesowen, Brighton & Hove Albion (two spells)

Billy Jones – known as 'Bullit' to the fans and 'The Tipton Slasher' to his fellow Black Country folk – was a rip-roaring, all-purpose centre-forward, whose main objective was to score goals, or at least try to by shooting at random, from any distance with either foot. He was only 5ft 6ins tall and weighed barely 12st, but he feared no one and spearheaded the Blues attack with great menace for eight years, and it was noticeable that the decline of the team in the late Edwardian era coincided with a series of injuries suffered by him, which kept him on the sidelines.

Born deep in the heart of the Black Country, Jones played for his local team Princes End before having spells with Smethwick Town and Halesowen, signing as a full-time professional for Blues in August 1901 – just in time to start a new campaign of First Division football following the club's promotion the season before. Surprisingly, despite having scored plenty of goals at non-League level over the previous two years, he went straight into Blues' second XI, and he had to fight for a place in the senior side owing to the form of Bob McRoberts and John McMillan. He had just four outings in 1901–02, scoring twice, on his debut against Sheffield United and in his next match versus Nottingham Forest.

Jones started 1902–03 in the Blues first team – but not as leader of attack. He was selected on the left wing and then had a few games as a wing-half then as an inside-forward and actually lined up in one fixture, against Barnsley, in the centre-half position. This was not what he wanted, but he stuck in there, and halfway through the following season, at long last, he was handed the centre-forward berth on a regular basis – and he never looked back. He scored eight goals that season (1903–04) and was leading marksman with 16 the following term, adding another 24 to his tally in 1905–06, helping Blues twice rise to seventh spot in the First Division table, their highest placing in the club's history at that juncture.

An ever present in 1906–07, when he was aided and abetted in attack by inside-forwards Benny Green and Arthur Mounteney, Jones was in the Blues side for their first ever match at St Andrew's against Middlesbrough on Boxing Day, and three days later he scored his first goal on the new ground against Preston, one of 15 he notched that season. Injuries interrupted his progress the following season and again in 1908–09 when he managed only 13 goals in total before he was transferred, perhaps surprisingly, to Southern League side Brighton & Hove Albion, Blues thinking he was past his best.

How wrong they were. Jones spent three seasons with Brighton and scored plenty of goals before Blues persuaded him to return to St Andrew's, paying £225 for his signature in April 1912. He rejuvenated the team to a certain extent, and with Jack Hall and George Robertson boldly assisting him in attack, he top scored with 16 goals in 1912–13 and went on to serve the club until November 1913 at which point he went back to Brighton. He played on through World War One and eventually announced his retirement in May 1920 to become assistant trainer of the Sussex-based club, a position he held for 19 years, although occasionally he did take over as head trainer.

Jones was 67 when he died in 1948 after a short illness. A relative of his, Abe Jones, played centre-half for West Bromwich Albion, Middlesbrough and Luton Town between 1897 and 1907.

Charlie Wilson Jones

Date of birth: 29 April 1914, Pentre Broughton near Wrexham
Died: 9 January 1986, Birmingham

Blues record:
Appearances: League 135, FA Cup 16, Wartime 65
Goals: League 63, FA Cup 8, Wartime 40
Debut: League, 1 September 1934 v Stoke City (a) lost 2–0

Also played for: Brymbo Green, Oswestry Town, Blackburn Rovers (trial), Bolton Wanderers (trial), Wrexham, guested for Blackpool, Huddersfield Town, West Bromwich Albion and Wrexham during World War Two, Nottingham Forest, Wrexham (again), Redditch United, Kidderminster Harriers, Wales (2 full caps)

After unsuccessful trials with two Lancashire clubs, Blackburn Rovers and Bolton Wanderers, centre-forward Charlie Wilson Jones joined Third Division North side Wrexham as an amateur in May 1932, turning professional three months later. A former cobbler, he spent two seasons at the Racecourse Ground before moving to St Andrew's in September 1934, signed for £1,500 by manager George Liddell, who had been mightily impressed with his initial performances for the Welsh club, for whom he scored four times in eight senior games as well as bagging plenty more goals for the second team in the Birmingham & District League.

A pale-faced, red haired, deceptively frail looking forward, Jones had a sterling rise to fame. Within a month of joining Blues he had made his debut in the First Division, and by late October he was a regular in the side, gaining the first of two full caps for Wales, scoring on his debut against Northern Ireland. His second cap came against France in 1939. He went on to top score with 17 goals for Blues that season, including a hat-trick in a 3–2 home League win over Derby County.

The following season Jones missed only three matches and rattled in another 20 goals (19 in the League), forming a fine understanding with Fred Harris and Frank White as Blues rose to 12th place in the table. And then, in 1936–37, he notched another eight goals in 22 starts before an injury forced him out of action. Annoyed at being sidelined, he went in for treatment twice a day, but he was out of the first team until September 1937, returning in style with a goal at Middlesbrough to earn his side a point.

Unfortunately Jones didn't look right, lacking his usual enthusiasm and endeavour. In fact, he made only 19 senior appearances that season, netting nine goals, and it was more of the same in the last campaign before World War Two, knee and ankle problems and a loss of form restricting him to just 21 League outings (six goals). His absence from half of the matches proved decisive as far as Blues were concerned as they slipped into the Second Division, due mainly to a lack of goals, which a fully fit and in form Jones would have provided.

At this juncture, Jones also lost popularity with the fans and was possibly the first Blues player to receive concerted barracking, but he quickly got over that, regained his full fitness during the war and went on to strike 40 goals in 65 wartime games for Blues, including 20 in 1945–46 when Blues won the Championship of the Football League South, pipping Aston Villa on goal average. He also assisted a handful of other clubs as a guest player, netting 40 goals for Blackpool during the early part of the hostilities.

When peacetime League football returned in 1946 Jones was immediately installed in the side at centre-forward, scoring five goals in nine games before another injury and a loss of form saw him replaced by Cyril Trigg.

In September 1947 Jones was transferred to Nottingham Forest, and after spells in non-League football with Redditch United and Kidderminster Harriers he announced his retirement in May 1950, at which time he entered into the licensing trade, where he continued until 1978. He was approaching his 72nd birthday when he died in 1986.

Jack Jones

Date of birth: 8 February 1891, Rotherham
Died: 20 July 1948, Rotherham

Blues record:
Appearances: League 228, FA Cup 9
Goals: League 1, FA Cup 0
Debut: League, 31 August 1920 v Hull City (h) won 5–1

Also played for: Allerton Bywater Colliery, Industry FC, Bird-in-Hand FC, Maltby Main Colliery, Army football (RAF), Sunderland, Nelson, Crewe Alexandra, Scarborough

Former Yorkshire miner Jack 'Cracker' Jones was one of the toughest left-backs in the League during the 1920s. A formidable defender, well built with a biting tackle, he was something special in the fact that he was as rough as his partner Frank Womack was fair. Opposing wingers rarely relished a confrontation with this muscular footballer, and it was certainly not surprising that he was often involved in disciplinary action. He actually played in dentures until one notable occasion, on a close season tour to Spain, when they were smashed as he took a full-blooded shot in the face, only to have a penalty for handball awarded against him!

Jones played all his early football in local Leagues in his native Yorkshire before joining Sunderland as a professional in November 1914. He served his country in the Army during World War One, but on his return to Wearside he failed to make headway and was confined to playing in the second team at Roker Park.

Looking for a replacement full-back, Blues secretary (and acting manager) Frank Richards was informed of the availability of Jones by a colleague in the north and after consulting his committee members at St Andrew's a meeting was arranged and the transfer went through, Blues paying £2,000 for his services in May 1920.

Jones made his League debut in the second match of the 1920–21 season against Hull City at St Andrew's when he partnered Womack for the first time, and what a partnership this turned out to be. These two players appeared together at full-back more than 180 times over the next seven years or so, helping Blues win the Second Division Championship in 1921 and rise to eighth position in the top flight – the club's highest placing since 1906.

A Football League representative versus the Scottish League in 1924–25, Jones – injuries and suspension apart – remained a regular in the Blues defence until October 1926, eventually losing his place to Percy Barton. He returned for the odd game here and there afterwards and made his final farewell appearance for the club in April 1927 against Leeds United at Elland Road (lost 2–1). In that Championship-winning season of 1920–21, he played in 37 League games and in 1921–22 – when Blues did not participate in the FA Cup owing to an error by the club's secretary who failed to submit an entry form – and missed only nine matches. In 1922–23 he was absent just once in a match against Liverpool at home, and the following season he played in just 22 League games, mainly due to injury. Back to full fitness in 1924–25, he again missed only one home match (against West Ham United), and he made 40 League appearances in 1925–26 and scored his only goal for Blues – the winner versus Manchester United at St Andrew's in April (2–1). This was unusual for him as he very rarely ventured over the halfway line, although when he did he loved to have a pop at goal, once striking the crossbar from 40 yards with a pile-driver against West Bromwich Albion at The Hawthorns in October 1924.

Jones was subsequently transferred to Nelson in May 1927. After 13 League appearances for the Lancashire club, he switched his allegiance to Crewe Alexandra in March 1928. He played in almost 100 first-class games for the Railwaymen (scoring seven goals) before ending his career with non-League side Scarborough, whom he served from September 1930 until his retirement in May 1931. He remained in the Yorkshire area for a few years after that, eventually returning to his home town of Rotherham where he died at the age of 57.

Howard Kendall

Date of birth: 22 May 1946, Ryton-on-Tyne

Blues record:
Appearances: League 115, FA Cup 9, League Cup 4, others 6
Goals: League 16, FA Cup 2, League Cup 0, others 0
Debut: League, 16 February 1974 v Wolverhampton Wanderers (a) lost 1–0

Also played for: Preston North End, Everton (2 spells, the second as player-manager), Stoke City, Blackburn Rovers (player-manager), England (6 Under-23 caps)
Managed: Everton, Athletic Bilbao (Spain), Manchester City, Xanthi (Greece), Notts County

Midfielder Howard Kendall rose to prominence when he became the youngest player (at that time) ever to appear in an FA Cup Final, lining up for Preston North End against West Ham in 1964 at the age of 17 years and 345 days, a record he lost to Paul Allen, ironically of West Ham, in 1980.

On 8 May 1981, Kendall became the youngest manager ever appointed by Everton, aged 34 years and 351 days. Voted Manager of the Year for 1984–85, after steering the Merseysiders to the First Division title and winning the European Cup-winners' Cup, he later added a second League Championship to his list of achievements (1987) and guided the Merseysiders to three successive Charity Shield victories as well as winning the FA Cup in 1985 and finishing runners-up in the same competition in 1985 and 1986.

Described as the 'complete midfielder', Kendall represented Ryton & District Schools and played for Wales at Schoolboy level before joining Preston as an apprentice in June 1961, turning professional in May 1963. Four years later, after making over 100 senior appearances for North End, he was transferred to Everton for £80,000 (March 1967) and the following year played in his second FA Cup Final when the Merseysiders lost 1–0 to West Bromwich Albion after extra-time. He also represented England at Under-23 level against Wales, the first of six caps in this category, although a full cap eluded him, quite why, no one knows! He did, however, play for the Football League.

Kendall teamed up exceedingly well with Colin Harvey and Alan Ball in Everton's engine room, becoming a firm favourite with the fans, who later took to him as a manager. He scored 29 goals in over 270 appearances for Everton in seven years, helping them win the League title in 1970 before moving down the M6 to join Blues in March 1974 as part of a complicated deal involving centre-forward Bob Latchford and full-back Archie Styles, Everton receiving £350,000 as their share of the three-player transaction.

Appointed captain of Blues, Kendall's experience and know-how went a long way in helping the club to retain its First Division status at the end of the 1973–74 season, courtesy of three draws and two wins from their final five matches, as they finished four points clear of the drop-zone. The following season he missed only three League games, helping Blues reach the semi-finals of the FA Cup, when they lost to Fulham after a replay. He was an absentee from six fixtures in 1975–76 and added 28 more appearances to his tally in 1976–77 before moving to Stoke City for £40,000. He spent two years at The Victoria Ground, making 91 appearances for the Potters before taking over as player-manager of Blackburn Rovers in June 1979, signed for £20,000. After guiding Rovers to the Third Division title in 1980, he returned to Goodison Park in the same capacity in May 1981, retiring as a player the following year with a record of 65 goals in 613 League appearances accumulated over a period of 19 years, serving with five different clubs.

Kendall continued as Everton manager until June 1987 when he took charge of Athletic Bilbao, retaining that position without success until November 1989. A month later he became boss of Manchester City, and in November 1990 he returned to Goodison Park for another spell as manager, remaining in office until December 1993. After that he managed Xanthi (May–November 1994) and Notts County (January–April 1995) before quitting top-class football for good.

Noel Kinsey

Date of birth: 24 December 1925, Treorchy, Glamorgan

Blues record:
Appearances: League 149, FA Cup 20, Europe 4+1
Goals: League 48, FA Cup 8, Europe 0
Debut: League, 19 August 1953 v Hull City (h) won 2–0

Also played for: Treorchy Amateurs, Cardiff City, Norwich City, Port Vale, Kings Lynn, Lowestoft, Wales (7 full caps)

Noel Kinsey signed initially for Cardiff City as a 14-year-old in the summer of 1941, turning professional at Ninian Park at the age of 17. Unfortunately, he never made the Bluebirds League side but did play in two wartime games. He remained with the Welsh club until June 1947 when he transferred to Norwich City for £3,000, linking up again with Cyril Spears, his former boss at Cardiff. Initially a wing-half, he later became a scheming inside-forward with the Canaries, full of inventiveness and constructive ideas, making openings galore for his colleagues with defence-splitting passes while still retaining a penchant for the surprise shot at goal himself. He was a roving opportunist, although he was never really regarded as an out-and-out striker.

Kinsey's form earned him the first of seven full caps for Wales in 1951 when he starred alongside Trevor Ford and Ivor Allchurch in the Home international match against Northern Ireland at Windsor Park, Belfast, performing well in a 2–1 win. He played against Portugal and Switzerland later that same year and also against England in 1952 before winning his other three caps as a Blues player versus Northern Ireland, England and Scotland between 1954 and 1956. He also represented the Football League against the Paris League in 1951.

Kinsey scored 65 times in 243 senior appearances for Norwich before moving to Blues in June 1953, signed by manager Arthur Turner for what was to prove a bargain fee of just under £4,000. Replacing Len Boyd, who was switched to the right-half position, he settled in quickly at St Andrew's, partnering Jackie Stewart on the right wing and making 37 appearances in his first season of Second Division football, netting 10 goals in the process, two coming in his first three matches. The following season he was outstanding as Blues won the Championship, thus regaining their top-flight status after a pause of five years. He netted 13 goals, including two braces, the first in a 4–0 home win over Ipswich Town and the second in a 7–2 crushing of his future club Port Vale, also at St Andrew's.

Blues reached the FA Cup Final for only the second time in the club's history in 1956, and Kinsey had the pleasure of scoring his side's equaliser against Manchester City, who went on to win the trophy 3–1 despite seeing their German goalkeeper Bert Trautmann break his neck in a collision with Blues' forward Peter Murphy. Blues finished a very creditable sixth in the First Division that season – their highest placing ever in the Football League, and Kinsey contributed 14 goals in 34 appearances, firing in a wonderful hat-trick in a 6–2 home win over Everton on Boxing Day. He also scored twice in the 4–0 win over Arsenal and in the 3–2 success versus Portsmouth, both at St Andrew's, and added six more goals to his League tally in 1956–57 (in 28 outings) when Blues came close to a Wembley FA Cup Final again, losing to Manchester United in the semis, but in February 1958 he moved on to pastures new, joining Port Vale after losing his place in the side to fellow Welshman Bryan Orritt. He became player-coach of the Potteries club and went on to net seven goals in 77 first-class appearances before switching to Kings Lynn after his release in April 1962. Later employed as player-coach by Lowestoft Town, he worked for the Norwich Union Insurance Company for several years and is currently living in the Norwich area, and he is believed to be one of Blues' oldest living former players.

Leslie Knighton

Date of birth:	12 March 1884, Church Gresley near Burton-on-Trent, Staffordshire
Died:	20 March 1959, Bournemouth

Blues record:

Manager:	August 1928 to May 1933
Played for:	Burton Town Boys, Gresley Rovers
Also managed:	Castleford Town, Arsenal, Chelsea, Shrewsbury Town

Blues appointed Leslie Knighton as team manager at the club's annual general meeting in July 1928 as successor to Billy Beer, and he took up his position a month later. A quiet man who rarely attended training sessions, allowing his assistant at the time to look after the players, he was nonetheless always available to give advice, there to sort out teething problems and to communicate with any member of the club's staff, players or otherwise. On match days he would enter the dressing room but hardly discussed tactics. People said he was 'too nice' to be a manager and some players took advantage of his casual approach, certainly on away trips which, in those days, regularly involved an overnight stay. Yet he became one of the best known and admired managers in the Football League, very popular with directors and even in the opposition changing rooms, which he usually visited on match days.

Knighton had been forced to retire as a player through injury in 1904 and accepted his first managerial post that same year with non-League side Castleford Town. After spells as an assistant manager at Huddersfield Town and Manchester City, he was appointed manager of Arsenal in 1919, shortly after the Gunners had been promoted to the First Division. He oversaw the club for six years, but the Londoners never finished higher than ninth during his tenure.

While at Highbury, Knighton was involved in one of the first recorded cases of doping. Before a January 1925 FA Cup tie against West Ham United, he gave his players what he described as 'little silver pills' which had been prescribed to him by a Harley Street doctor who was a supporter of the club. Although the pills were successful in increasing the players' energy levels, after three matches they rebelled and refused to take them for fear of ill effects. These activities, entirely legal under the rules at the time, were not made public until he recounted the episode in his memoirs.

Unfortunately Knighton had numerous fallings-out with the Arsenal chairman Sir Henry Norris, who put a strict cap of £1,000 on all transfer fees and refused to sign any player under 5ft 8in tall or less than 11 stones in weight. However, when he signed the 5ft tall Hugh 'Midget' Moffatt from Workington in 1923, Norris was furious. Norris immediately confronted him and promptly sold the player to Luton Town before he'd played a League game. However, despite Norris's interfering, he signed several quality players for Arsenal, including Bob John and Jimmy Brain, but he could never knit together a solid, winning side and the team's performances gradually declined towards the end of his tenure. The Gunners finished 19th in 1923–24 and 20th the following season.

Knighton was dismissed in the summer of 1925, and it was alleged that Norris only sacked him to avoid paying him a bonus from a benefit match that he was due. Norris denied this and instead cited Leslie's poor managerial record, but later regretted his dismissal and in his will left Knighton £100, a substantial sum at that time.

Knighton built up a fine side at St Andrew's, bringing in one or two quality players, among them Ned Barkas, whom he knew at Huddersfield, to go with those already established in the side. He guided Blues to the 1931 FA Cup Final (beaten by West Bromwich Albion 2–1) and remained in charge at St Andrew's until the summer of 1933, when he took over the reins at Stamford Bridge, Chelsea making him an offer he couldn't refuse. He remained with the London club for six years, helping them avoid relegation from the First Division.

Following a period of ill-health, Knighton managed Shrewsbury Town in the Midland League for a short time before retiring in 1941. He later became secretary of a Bournemouth golf club and was 75 when he died in 1959.

Bob Latchford

Date of birth: 18 January 1951, Kings Heath, Birmingham

Blues record:
Appearances: League 158+2, FA Cup 11, League 15+2, others 6
Goals: League 68, FA Cup 6, League 6, others 4
Debut: League, 22 March 1969 v Preston North End (h) won 3–1

Also played for: Everton, Swansea City, NAC Breda (Holland), Coventry City, Lincoln City, Newport County (loan), Merthyr Tydfil, England (12 full, 6 Under-21 caps)

Centre-forward Bob Latchford attended and played for Brandwood Secondary School and represented South Birmingham and Warwickshire County Schools before joining Blues as an apprentice in May 1967, turning professional in August 1968. Making excellent progress at St Andrew's via the intermediate, reserve and youth teams, gaining an FA Youth Cup runners'-up medal in 1967 and winning four youth caps for England, he celebrated by scoring twice on his League debut against Preston North End in March 1969, when manager Stan Cullis selected him following an injury to Dave Robinson, which resulted in Kenny Burns switching back into a defence position. He made three more appearances that season and 11 (one goal) in 1969–70 before gaining a regular place in the side the following season when he partnered Phil Summerill and Trevor Francis up front, ending up with 13 goals.

Despite his bulky physique, Latchford was surprisingly agile, strong in the air with a powerful right-foot shot. He was also quick over short distances and proved to be handful for any defender in and around the penalty area. In 1971–72 he was in sparkling form, cracking in 27 goals, 23 coming in the League, as Blues clinched promotion by taking the runners'-up spot in Division Two. His haul included two hat-tricks in the space of 24 days in September, in 4–1 home wins over Charlton Athletic and Watford, and he also netted in six successive games during October and November. He maintained his form in the top flight, top scoring with 19 goals (20 in total) as Blues consolidated themselves in 10th position.

Now recognised as a quality striker, in 1973–74 Latchford represented England in three Under-23 internationals, later doubling that tally and also playing for the senior side. He also struck another 17 goals before bidding farewell to the St Andrew's faithful, joining Everton in the February in a complex deal that involved two other players and £350,000. Howard Kendall moved to Blues while full-back Archie Styles went with Latchford to Goodison Park. With the Merseysiders, his game improved even more. Taking over from Joe Royle, he scored seven times in his first 13 games for Everton, played in the losing 1977 League Cup Final against Aston Villa, and in 1977–78 he was presented with a cheque for £10,000 by a national newspaper after becoming the first player to net 30 goals in Division One for six years, clinching the prize money with a brace in the very last match of the season against Chelsea.

Latchford went on to become Everton's highest post-war goalscorer, amassing a total of 138 in 289 games and finishing up as leading marksman five seasons running between 1974 and 1979. Leaving Goodison Park for Swansea City in a £125,000 deal in July 1981, he gained a Welsh Cup-winners' medal at the end of his first season at the Vetch Field but failed to make much of an impact with his next club Dutch side NAC Breda, whom he served for just four months from February 1984. He returned to England to net twice in 14 outings for Coventry City during the 1984–85 season before winding down his League career with spells at Lincoln City and Newport County, serving both clubs during the 1985–86 campaign. He finally ended up with Merthyr Tydfil, collecting a second Welsh Cup-winners' medal in 1987. Bob later became a director of Alvechurch FC.

Latchford's playing career spanned more than 20 years, and in that time he netted over 280 goals in more than 650 senior appearances. He also scored five goals in 12 full internationals for England between 1977 and 1979, and he also represented the Football League XI. His brothers were both professional goalkeepers, Dave with Blues, Motherwell, Bury, Barnsley and Cheltenham Town and Peter with West Bromwich Albion, Celtic and Clyde.

Dave Latchford

Date of birth: 9 April 1949, Kings Heath, Birmingham

Blues record:
Appearances: League 206, FA Cup 14, League Cup 10, others 9
Goals: 0
Debut: League, 8 April 1969 v Bury (a) won 2–1

Also played for: Motherwell, Bury, Barnsley, Redditch United, Cheltenham Town, East Worle

Like his brothers, Bob and Peter, Dave Latchford attended and played for Brandwood Secondary Modern School and also represented South Birmingham Schools before joining Blues as an apprentice in June 1964, turning professional in May 1966, gaining an FA Youth Cup runners'-up medal a year later (with brother Bob). He was also a member of the England Youth squad for the 1967 European Youth tournament in Turkey but failed to gain a place due to the brilliance of a certain Peter Shilton. He eventually followed his brother Bob into the Blues first team at the end of the 1968–69 season, making his debut 24 hours before his 20th birthday in a 2–1 League win at Bury in front of just 5,819 hardy supporters. Three days later over 53,000 fans saw him in action in the Birmingham derby at Villa Park, a game Blues lost 1–0.

Taking over between the posts on a regular basis from Scotsman Jim Herriot in February 1970, Latchford then had to battle to keep his first-team place following the arrival of Mike Kelly, and for a period of time he had to play second fiddle to the former England amateur international, whom he finally dislodged halfway through Blues' 1971–72 promotion-winning campaign in Division Two, only for Paul Cooper to step forward as well.

At this juncture, Blues manager Freddie Goodwin was ready to listen to offers for 'Big Dave' but the 'keeper stayed put and bided his time in the reserves. Goodwin pointed out 'He came into the side when the chips were down and did everything that was asked of him. It was a big decision to leave him out, but I believe he benefitted from his experience.' Latchford stated 'If I had been playing as well as young Paul was, I would not have expected to have had to stand down. But that's football. We shared a great respect for each other, as do most goalkeepers.'

Despite his bulky appearance, Latchford was surprisingly agile, and he was also a clean handler of the ball, possessing the ability to make the occasional impossible save. He certainly produced the goods during the second half of the 1971–72 season when he and Cooper shared the goalkeeping duties. In fact, he conceded only four goals in nine appearances. Once in the top flight, he finally became Blues' first-choice 'keeper, and he kept his place and maintained his form right through to the end of the 1976–77 League programme.

In 1975 he was bitterly disappointed when Blues lost to Fulham in an FA Cup semi-final replay and was annoyed further when manager Willie Bell signed Jim Montgomery to take over the number-one position in February 1977. He slipped into the reserves, coming back for two games late on before leaving St Andrew's that summer, signing for the Scottish First Division club Motherwell after conceding eight goals in his own testimonial match! In March 1979 he returned to England with Bury, and after assisting Barnsley as a non-contract player in 1980 he then ventured into non-League football with Redditch United in 1981 and then Cheltenham Town two years later. His final two clubs were East Worle, whom he served from 1985, and Solihull Borough, engaged by the latter as senior coach for three years from August 1992 to June 1995.

After being employed for a number of years as a funeral director, Latchford became a superintendent of cemeteries for Solihull, while his son Oliver played for Solihull Borough and the West Midlands Police team.

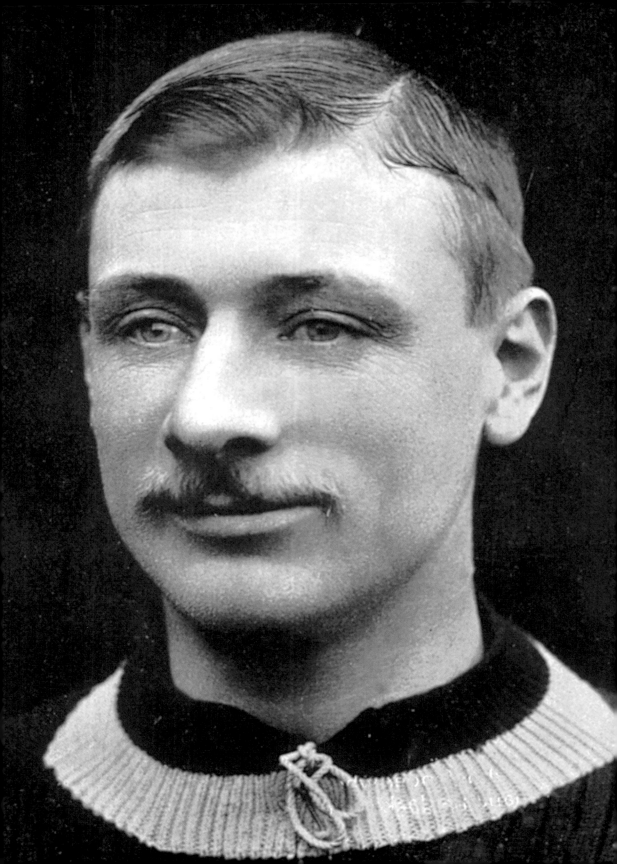

Alex Leake

Date of birth: 11 July 1871, Small Heath, Birmingham
Died: 29 March 1938, Birmingham

Blues record:
Appearances: League 199, FA Cup 18, Test Matches 4
Goals: League 21, FA Cup 2, Test Matches 0
Debut: League, 5 October 1895 v Preston North End (a) lost 3–2

Also played for: Hoskins & Sewell FC (two spells), Kings Heath Albion, Saltley Gas Works FC, Singers FC (Coventry), Old Hill Wanderers, Aston Villa, Burnley, Wednesbury Old Athletic, England (5 full caps)

Centre-half Alex Leake was educated in Bordesley Green and played for several local intermediate clubs before joining Blues as a full-time professional in the summer of 1894, just 48 hours after his 23rd birthday.

Playing football was a pleasure for Leake. He would crack a joke with an opponent while robbing him of the ball, chunter and chit-chat to the opposition in a crowded penalty area waiting for a corner-kick to be sent over and even carry out a lengthy conversation with the referee or a linesman when there was a pause in play. He skippered Blues for six years, and he was good at his job.

A genuine 'Brummagem Button' with a dapper moustache and smartly-groomed hair, Leake was a good tempered, honest defender, whose stamina was unsurpassed. He never played to the gallery but always battled well for his team, no matter what the circumstances – a fighter to the last. He was as safe as houses, never overdoing the fancy stuff, and was always hard to beat in 50–50 situations. As well as being an exceptionally fine tackler, he was superb at intercepting long passes, he could head a ball hard and true and kick long and straight. He was, at times, a star performer, and without doubt his unfamiliar humour made him a great favourite with the fans and his colleagues alike.

After making his League debut for Blues at left-half at Preston in October 1895, later that season Leake gained a regular place in the team at centre-half, taking over the duties from Harry Haynes, and he was the fourth player used in the central-defensive position that season, the other two being Ted Jolly and Billy Walton. He appeared in 14 League games in 1895–96, scoring his first goal for the club in a 1–1 home draw with Sheffield Wednesday. Unfortunately his efforts were all in vain as Blues slipped into the Second Division after losing two and drawing one of their four Test Matches at the end of the campaign.

Now firmly bedded in as Blues number-one pivot – and unchallenged – the following season Leake was an ever present as Blues finished fourth in Division Two. In 1897–98 he missed just two League games, participated in all 34 in 1898–99, and then in 1899–1900 he missed five matches while also being pushed forward as Blues battled for promotion. He netted eight goals during that campaign, including two in a 6–0 home win over Loughborough. However, again his efforts went unrewarded as Blues missed out on promotion, finishing third in the table. He spent two more seasons with Blues, adding a further 70 senior appearances to his tally, which stood at 221 when he transferred to Aston Villa in June 1902. Two years later he won the first of five full caps for England, lining up against Ireland. He was never on the losing side at international level, and he also represented the Football League.

In 1905 Leake gained a League Championship-winners' medal and went on to appear in 141 matches for Villa before joining Burnley in December 1907. Quitting top-class football at the end of the 1909–10 season with 464 senior appearances under his belt, he returned to the Midlands as a player with Wednesbury Old Athletic, retiring in May 1912.

Two months later he was appointed trainer-coach at Crystal Palace and in an emergency was chosen as a reserve for the England team at the age of 41. He then served as trainer-coach at Merthyr Town from October 1919 before spending a season as head trainer with Walsall in September 1932 to May 1933. He later coached at schools and colleges around Britain for six years. Besides his footballing exploits, he was an excellent swimmer who would dive to the bottom of the brine baths at Droitwich to retrieve a coin. He was also a track athlete, specialising in the 400 yards and hurdles events. The cousin of Blues' Jimmy Windridge, he was a keen gardener and a blacksmith by trade.

George Liddell

Date of birth: 14 July 1895, Durham
Died: Winter 1970, Hampshire

Blues record:
Appearances: League 323, FA Cup 22
Goals: League 6, FA Cup 0
Debut: League, 28 August 1920 v South Shields (a) lost 3–0
Manager: August 1933–September 1939

Also played for: Honourable Artillery Company XI, Duke of Wellington FC, Yorkshire Amateurs, South Shields

A pupil at the Johnstone Grammar School (Durham) and also at the City of Leeds Training College, George Liddell joined the Army in 1909, and besides playing football during his national service he also participated in rugby union. After his demob, he signed for Yorkshire Amateurs and thereafter had a decent spell with South Shields before joining Blues as a full-time professional in May 1920. He spent the next 12 years at St Andrew's, retiring in April 1932. Fourteen months later he took over as Blues' manager from Leslie Knighton, who had moved to Chelsea, and retained his position until May 1939.

During his early playing career Liddell occupied the right-half position, and he made his League debut in place of the injured Jack Roulson on the opening day of Blues' Second Division promotion-winning campaign of 1920–21 against his former club South Shields. He continued to play in that position (right-half) for several years, as well as having a few outings here and there on the opposite flank. He scored the first of his six League goals for the club in a 3–0 home win over Oldham Athletic in December 1921 and followed up four months later with a strike that earned an away point from a 1–1 draw with rivals Aston Villa. His other four goals were scored at Sheffield United in March 1925 (lost 4–3), away to Sheffield Wednesday in April 1927 (drew 4–4), against Leeds United at home in December 1928 (won 5–1) and against Huddersfield Town at St Andrew's in September 1929 (won 4–1).

During the 1927–28 campaign Liddell started to have a few games at right-back and the following season his outings were divided between the full-back and wing-half berths. It wasn't until November 1929 that he finally established himself in the right-back position as partner to skipper Ned Barkas, taking over the duties previously carried out by Frank Womack and England international Joe Smith. George and Barkas developed a fine understanding with each other, and the following season they lined up in the FA Cup Final at Wembley when Blues took on Midlands neighbours West Bromwich Albion on a sodden pitch. He played well against Albion's flying left-winger Stan Wood, but in the end it was the Baggies who came out on top, winning 2–1.

Cool under pressure, Liddell was a fine positional player, possessing a powerful right-footed kick and strong tackle, and he could always be relied upon to give a solid performance, no matter who his opponent might be. He prompted his forwards well, especially from the wing-half spot, his skills shining through above the average player occupying a similar position. A defender who preferred to pass the ball rather than lash it blindly downfield, in later years he combined football with a career as a teacher with the result that he frequently missed mid-week away matches.

Unfortunately, Liddell was not the most popular of players with his teammates, and it was certainly a big surprise when he was handed the manager's job by Blues chairman Harry Morris – although it was public knowledge that he had always stated that he wanted to manage the club. Indeed, there was considerable dressing room rancour throughout his managerial career, although he did a useful job in difficult circumstances, his youth policy producing a string of fine footballers. However, after a few near misses in the relegation stakes, George was eventually dismissed in May 1939 when Blues lost their First Division status after 18 years.

Soon after leaving St Andrew's, Liddell – who by now was well into his 40s – became an English teacher at Leigh Road School, Washwood Heath and then at Cotteridge Infants School near Kings Heath before taking over as headmaster of Handsworth Grammar School – all in Birmingham. He moved to Hampshire in the early 1960s and was 75 when he died.

Alexander McClure

Date of birth: 3 April 1892, Workington, Cumbria
Died: 12 August 1973, Birmingham

Blues record:
Appearances: League 192, FA Cup 6, Wartime 48
Goals: League 4, FA Cup 0, Wartime 2
Debut: League, 27 January 1912 v Stockport County (h) won 2–0

Also played for: Grangetown Juniors (two spells), South Bank, Bellis & Morcom (guest), Aston Villa, Stoke, Coventry City,
Walsall, Luton Town (player-coach), Bromsgrove Rovers (player-coach), Market Harborough Town
Managed: Birmingham (Colts team)

Centre-half Alec McClure was blessed with a fine physique and excellent positional sense. He was the fulcrum of the Blues defence for 12 years, during which time – injuries permitting – he appeared in almost 200 first-class matches. Very few forwards relished a run-in with the powerful northerner from the Lake District, whose solid tackling and bone-shaking shoulder charges earned him a great reputation among the Blues supporters – but not so with the opposing players!

McClure skippered Blues' second XI to victory in three major competitions and made his entry into League football against Stockport County in January 1912 before establishing himself in the first team at St Andrew's during the 1912–13 campaign, when he shared the centre-half berth with Alf Tinkler. The following season he appeared in 18 League and Cup games before an injury allowed Tinkler back into the side. On regaining full fitness, he made only four starts in the last season before World War One, and during the hostilities – when he served in the Royal Navy, participating in the Zeebrugge Affair, one of the great military actions of World War One – he appeared in almost 50 regional games, helping Blues win the Midland Section Subsidiary tournament and finish second in the Midland Section Principal competition in 1919.

Back to his best in the 1919–20 season when he made 26 senior appearances, McClure then had a major input as Blues won the Second Division Championship the following season. He missed only two League matches, the defeat at South Shields and a 3–0 win at Stockport, and netted two goals, a priceless winner at home to Leeds United on New Year's Day (1–0) and the clincher in a 3–0 victory in the local derby against Wolves at St Andrew's.

Retaining his place in the first team throughout the next two campaigns, when he missed only 11 games, all due to injury, McClure came under pressure from a number of defenders who wanted his position in 1923–24, among them Dicky Dale and Jimmy Cringan. In the end he was replaced by Cringan, at which point (December 1923) he was transferred across the city to Aston Villa, who recruited him as experienced cover for George Blackburn and Dr Vic Milne. Villa reached the FA Cup Final that season (beaten 2–0 by Newcastle United), but unfortunately he didn't make the team at Wembley, sitting in the stand instead.

McClure made only seven League appearances in a little over 10 months at Villa Park, having a blinder in a 4–2 win at Liverpool in front of 45,000 fans in August 1924, before moving to Stoke, for whom he played in 31 games, later adding 51 more to his tally with Coventry City (7 goals) and starring in 11 senior matches for Walsall. He failed to make the first XI at Luton Town, being mainly engaged as a coach. He then served in the same capacity with non-League side Bromsgrove Rovers and also assisted Market Harborough Town before returning to St Andrew's as youth-team coach in August 1928. He acted as Birmingham's assistant manager for two years from May 1932 to April 1934, first to Leslie Knighton and then to George Liddell. In fact, he was in line to take over as manager when Knighton left, but in the end his former teammate was given the job. During those two years he kept fit by continuing to play regularly for Market Harborough.

On retiring from football in the mid-1930s McClure took employment with the Rudge Motor Cycle company while also running his own haulage business in Small Heath, Birmingham. He saw his last live Blues game in 1967 and was 81 years of age when he died.

Ray Martin

Date of birth: 23 January 1945, Wolverhampton

Blues record:
Appearances: League 324+8, FA Cup 18+1, League Cup 18+1, others 4
Goals: League 1, FA Cup 0, League Cup 0, others 0
Debut: League, 11 January 1964 v Manchester United (a) won 2–1

Also played for: Aston Villa (juniors), Portland Timber (NASL), Minnesota Kicks (NASL)

During a morning's training session at Villa Park, a young amateur footballer by the name of Ray Martin broke a bone in the left foot of his manager Joe Mercer in a tackle. Within a matter of two weeks he was released by the club, but I am certain that the two incidents were not related – unless someone knows otherwise!

Martin, who represented South-East Staffordshire schoolboys as a 15-year-old, failed to make the first team during his only season with Aston Villa, and after joining Blues, initially as an apprentice in June 1961, moving up the ladder to the professional ranks in May 1962, he was carefully nurtured along before making an impressive League debut in place of Welsh international Colin Green in front of 44,695 spectators at Old Trafford, helping Blues, the League Cup holders, beat the FA Cup winners of 1963 Manchester United by two goals to one.

Martin held his place in the side at left-back for the next four games and was then switched to the right flank when Green returned and Stan Lynn was out injured. He went on to make 14 appearances that season, following up with 20 in 1964–65 when he also had two outings as an emergency inside-right at the end of a disastrous campaign which saw Blues relegated to the Second Division.

First choice in 1965–66, mainly as left-back with 'Cammy' Fraser as his partner, Martin also played in the first 19 League games of 1966–67 before suffering an injury against Carlisle United at Brunton Park, replaced by converted winger Bert Murray. He returned later for the home leg of the League Cup semi-final with Queen's Park Rangers but did not regain his first-team place until February 1968 – just in time to appear in the 2–0 FA Cup semi-final defeat by West Bromwich Albion at his former home Villa Park. Now occupying the left-back position and partnered by Murray, he made 32 appearances that season (six as a substitute) and followed up with 38 in 1968–69 when he played on the right side of the defence, with Colin Green returning on the left flank. England international Bobby Thomson then joined Blues from Wolverhampton Wanderers, and he teamed up with Ray to form Blues' full-back duo in 1969–70. He was superb throughout that season and scored his first and only goal for the club in a 4–2 home defeat by Hull City in the April. He was subsequently voted Blues Player of the Year. However, halfway through the 1971–72 campaign Ray lost his place to Irishman Tommy Carroll, although he did eventually appear in enough matches to receive a runners'-up medal as Blues clinched promotion back to the First Division.

During the next four seasons Martin – a player who always gave the impression he was thoroughly enjoying his football, his trademark being an amazing sliding tackle – made almost 120 first-class appearances for Blues, pushing his overall tally towards the 375 mark. He played with several new partners including Tony Want, Joe Gallagher, Dennis Clarke, Archie Styles and Steve Bryant, and he also enjoyed a loan spell in the North American Soccer League with Portland Timbers from May to August 1975, signing permanently for the club in May 1976 after losing out altogether to the newly-formed partnership of Page and Styles at Birmingham.

Early in 1979 Martin switched NASL clubs, joining forces with Minnesota Kicks, and after retiring later that same year he became a soccer coach at Oregon State University. Still a football lover, watching matches live and on TV whenever possible, he still resides in the US today.

Gil Merrick

Date of birth: 26 January 1922, Sparkhill, Birmingham

Blues record:
Appearances: League 485, FA Cup 56, Europe 10, Wartime 164
Goals: 0
Debut: Wartime, 20 May 1940 v Leicester City (h) drew 0–0
Senior debut: FA Cup, 5 January 1946 v Portsmouth (h) won 1–0
Manager: May 1960–June 1964

Also played for: Shirley Juniors, Army PTC, Solihull Town, England (23 caps)
Also managed: Bromsgrove Rovers, Atherstone Town

Regarded as one of the best goalkeepers in Great Britain during the early 1950s, Gil Merrick had the misfortune to be between the posts when the Hungarians put 13 goals past England in home and away internationals in 1953 and 1954, but he was hardly to blame for that barrage and soon afterwards played in the World Cup Finals in Switzerland.

It is said that Merrick copied the style of Harry Hibbs, his illustrious predecessor in the Birmingham goal. Certainly there were many similarities between the two 'keepers, Merrick being calm and unspectacular with a technique all of his own, that of tremendous positional sense. He also used the whole framework of his body to stop shots as well as having a massive pair of hands.

Born deep in Blues territory at Sparkhill in 1922, Merrick started playing football at the age of 10 and became a goalkeeper two years later. After serving with a handful of local junior clubs he joined Blues as an amateur in 1938 but was farmed out to gain competitive experience with Solihull Town just prior to the outbreak of World War Two, signing as a professional at St Andrew's in readiness for the ill-fated 1939–40 campaign, which was abandoned after most clubs had completed three League games.

Playing when he could during the hostilities, he assisted Blues in more than 160 regional games and was in tip-top form when recognised League football recommenced in August 1946.

A powerfully-built man with a dapper moustache, Merrick made well over 700 appearances for Blues, including wartime competitions, and, in fact, is the club's record appearance maker at senior level (551 games). Over a period of eight years, from August 1946 until April 1954, he was very rarely absent from competitive match action, only international duties and the occasional injury disrupting his progress, and he missed only 20 out of a possible 336 League games. He was an ever present twice in successive seasons of 1949–50 and 1950–51, failed to appear in only one game in each of the 1946–47, 1948–49 and 1951–52 campaigns and was absent twice in 1956–57.

Merrick helped Blues win the Football League South title in 1945–46, conceded only 24 goals in 41 League matches when the Second Division Championship was won in 1948–49, gained another Division Two winners' medal in 1955 and a year later did his utmost in trying to prevent Manchester City from winning the FA Cup, Blues eventually losing 3–1 at Wembley.

Between November 1951 and June 1954 Merrick gained 23 full caps for England, the first in a 2–0 win over Northern Ireland, the last in a 4–2 defeat by Uruguay in the World Cup Finals. England remained unbeaten in his first 12 internationals and lost five of his last 11. He kept five clean sheets and was eventually replaced by Ray Wood of Manchester United. He also represented the Football League on 11 occasions between 1947 and 1954, playing against the Irish League five times and the League of Ireland and the Scottish League three times each. In 1945–46 he played for the Army Physical Training team.

During his 13 years with Birmingham Merrick became a consistent performer in the side, but he was eventually replaced by Johnny Schofield in April 1959, having just two more outings the following season, announcing his retirement as a player in 1960. At that juncture – June 1960 – he was appointed manager at St Andrew's, and what a terrific first season he had in charge, leading Blues to the Inter Cities Fairs Cup Final. Two years later he celebrated again as Blues won the Football League Cup, defeating arch-rivals Aston Villa 3–1 over two legs in the Final.

Merrick remained in office for four years, and after leaving the club he took charge of Bromsgrove Rovers, later acting as manager of Atherstone Town during the late 1960s. He now lives in Shirley having worked for S&U at Solihull for may years.

Frank Mitchell

Date of birth: 3 June 1922, Goulburn, New South Wales, Australia
Died: 2 April 1984, Lapworth, Warwickshire

Blues record:
Appearances: League 93, FA Cup 13, Wartime 60
Goals: League 6, FA Cup 2, Wartime 2
Debut: Football League North, 4 September 1943 v Coventry City (h) lost 2–1
Senior debut: FA Cup, 5 January 1946 v Portsmouth (h) won 1–0

Also played for: Coventry City (amateur), wartime guest for Arsenal, Northampton Town and Portsmouth, Chelsea, Watford

Frank Rollason Mitchell first donned a Blues shirt in September 1943 when he played in the centre-half position against his former club Coventry City in a Wartime Football League North game before less than 8,000 spectators. Three years later he played in front of 10 times that number of fans when Blues lost their FA Cup semi-final replay 4–0 to Derby County at Maine Road, Manchester.

Mitchell appeared in several regional League and Cup games during the hostilities, helping Blues win the League South Championship in the transitional season of 1945–46 when he performed majestically at left-half in a middle line that also comprised his future manager Arthur Turner and the long-serving Fred Harris. He was also twice named as a reserve for the full England team in each of those first two post-war campaigns.

A very positive player, Mitchell, who was born and bred in Australia, had set his sights on spending his sporting career in cricket, and, in fact, he was a regular member of his local team in New South Wales – before he and his parents emigrated to England when he was in his early teens.

At the age of 15 Mitchell joined the groundstaff of Warwickshire County Cricket Club and at the same time, unsure of where he would go from there, he also signed as an amateur for Coventry City Football Club, playing in the Sky Blues Combination side before switching his allegiance to Blues in September 1943, while at the same time he was also making steady progress as a cricketer as well as playing as a guest for Arsenal, Northampton Town and the FA Cup holders Portsmouth when on leave from the Royal Navy. He also represented the FA XI against the APTC XI in 1945–46.

When the war was over, Mitchell delivered the goods in the left-half position in competitive football for Blues, scoring four goals in 43 senior appearances in 1946–47 and netting the same number in 42 outings the following season when Blues won the Second Division title after an 11-match unbeaten run at the end of their League programme, when the defence – which read Gil Merrick, Ken Green and Dennis Jennings, Fred Harris, Ted Duckhouse and Mitchell – performed superbly well, conceding only four goals and letting in just 24 in their 42 games overall.

A fine positional player, strong and precise with his kicking, Mitchell was a smart penalty taker, choosing to slide the ball into the net nonchalantly rather than give it a good, old-fashioned thump, but unfortunately he missed out as Blues attempted to establish themselves in the top flight. He missed the opening 13 matches and appeared in 11 of the next 12 before being transferred to Chelsea in January 1949, signed by manager Billy Birrell, who was looking to strengthen his defence. He remained at Stamford Bridge until August 1952 when he moved to Third Division South side Watford, with whom he remained until announcing his retirement in May 1958.

On the cricket front, Mitchell – who had trials for Kent and assisted Cornwall and Hertfordshire – played in 17 County matches for Warwickshire between 1946 and 1948, taking 22 wickets at an average of 38.9. He later scored a century at the age of 47 for Knowle & Dorridge Cricket Club before becoming secretary. He was also in charge of the sports grounds and coaching facilities at Kynoch's works, Birmingham, for many years.

Jim Montgomery

Date of birth: 9 October 1943, Sunderland

Blues record:
Appearances: League 66, FA Cup 2, League Cup 2, others 3
Goals: 0
Debut: League, 12 March 1977 v Derby County (a) drew 0–0

Also played for: Sunderland (two spells), Southampton (loan) Nottingham Forest, England (4 Youth, 6 Under-23 caps)

Goalkeeper Jim Montgomery made over 150 more appearances for Sunderland than any other player – totalling 627 during his two spells with the club from June 1958 to February 1977 and August 1980 to July 1982. He later returned to Roker Park as youth-team coach (1993) and went on to become director of youth coaching at the Stadium of Light. Known as 'Mighty Jim', he has been marked down as the greatest of all Sunderland goalkeepers, and because of his terrific record he also comes pretty high up on the Blues' list as well. His quite outstanding double-save from efforts by Trevor Cherry and then Peter Lorimer of Leeds United in the 1973 FA Cup Final at Wembley is regarded as the best individual feat achieved by a 'keeper at Wembley in any competition – and of course he helped his side lift the trophy.

Montgomery came close to gaining England recognition, but with Gordon Banks, Peter Bonetti and Alex Stepney around he was always in reserve, although he did make Sir Alf Ramsey's original 40-man squad for the 1970 World Cup Finals in Mexico – and one feels that if he had been included in the final 22 the World Cup would have been retained! As we know, Banks was sidelined for the crucial semi-final clash with West Germany, and Bonetti took over, but after holding a two-goal lead England lost 3–2. Many at the time – especially thousands of Sunderland fans – said that Montgomery should have been included, and he remains to this day as England's greatest uncapped goalkeeper. The nearest he got to playing for his country at senior level was against France in 1969 when he sat on the bench as an unused substitute. He did, however, gain six Under-23 caps and played for the Youth team.

Montgomery made his League debut for Sunderland at the age of 17, was an ever present four times and helped them gain promotion in 1964. He was released by the Wearside club at the age of 33 when he joined Blues in February 1977 after loan spells with Southampton, and he spent two and a half seasons at St Andrew's, during which time he appeared in 73 senior games for Blues. He replaced Dave Latchford between the posts, making his debut in a goalless draw at Derby just 24 hours after signing. He competently held his position in the side and made 12 appearances that season, followed by 43 in League and Cup competitions in 1977–78 when Blues finished 11th in the First Division. Still agile and courageous, he produced some brilliant performances, especially against Everton at home in December 1977, when Blues drew 0–0, and against Aston Villa in the local derby at St Andrew's in February 1978, when Trevor Francis's goal earned Blues a 1–0 win.

In 1978–79 Montgomery played in a struggling side as Blues hovered around the relegation zone, eventually falling through the trapdoor in 21st place. He appeared in 13 of the 42 League games that term, future policeman Neil Freeman participating in the other 29, and in August 1979, at the age of 38, he was signed by Nottingham Forest manager Brian Clough, going on to collect an European Cup-winners' medal (as a non-playing substitute) in 1980.

Montgomery returned to St Andrew's as a temporary coach in July 1980, but within a month he left the club and became player-coach back at Sunderland, later taking over as manager of the second team, a position he retained until July 1982. Some years later he was asked again to join Sunderland, this time as director of youth training at the club's new ground, the Stadium of Light. He now works for the club behind the scenes, hosting a 'Legends' table in the banqueting suite before every home game.

George Morrall

Date of birth: 4 October 1905, Smethwick
Died: 15 November 1955, Birmingham

Blues record:
Appearances: League 243, FA Cup 23
Goals: League 5, FA Cup 2
Blues debut: League, 24 December 1927 v Derby County (a) lost 1–4

Also played for: Gorse Street Primitive Methodists, Chance's Glassworks, Littleton Harriers, Allen Everitt's Sports, West Bromwich Albion (trial), Swindon Town

George 'Lofty' Morrall was a commanding figure in the centre of the Blues' defence for many years. He dominated in the air, was reliable, strong and solid on the ground, his tackling could be ferocious at times, and, above all, he possessed the heart of a lion, never failing to give 100 percent out on the field of play. A true professional, he produced some sterling performances for Blues, whom he served honestly for over nine years, amassing 266 senior appearances and scoring seven goals.

After playing for several local teams and having an unproductive trial with his boyhood heroes West Bromwich Albion, whom he first saw play in 1914, Morrall joined Blues as a professional in March 1927. He worked his socks off in the reserves for a season and a half before establishing himself as a member of the first team in 1929, taking over at centre-half from Jimmy Cringan, with George Liddell and Alec Leslie alongside him in what was a pretty effective middle line in front of two excellent full-backs in Ned Barkas and Jack Randle. He made 32 appearances in his first two seasons at St Andrew's before making 40 in 1929–30, when he also netted his first goals in League and FA Cup competitions. His effort against Bolton Wanderers was enough to bring Blues a 1–0 home win in the third round of the Cup, and three months later his net-buster earned his side a point from a 1–1 draw at Newcastle.

In 1930–31 Morrall was outstanding, helping Blues reach the FA Cup Final after ousting Liverpool, Port Vale, Watford, Chelsea and Sunderland, completely nullifying the threat of several quality international strikers, including the South African-born centre-forward Gordon Hodgson of Liverpool, who won caps for England, Chelsea's powerhouse George Mills and Bob Gurney of Sunderland, whose manager Johnny Cochrane said, after his side had been beaten 2–0 in the semi-final, 'Morrall's display was one of the best I have ever seen from a centre-half. He won everything in the air.' He played his heart out against the Baggies in the Final, but in the end he had to settle for a runners'-up medal as Blues went down 2–1 on a rain-soaked pitch.

Morrall, who was in line for an England call-up at this stage in his career, made 37 League and two Cup appearances in 1931–32 when Lew Stoker joined him in the half-back line, and the following season he missed just four League matches, all through injury. Around this time he was receiving treatment on his right knee, but he battled hard and long to get fit for the weekend matches, and in 1933–34 he made 31 starts out of a possible 45, bagging his second FA Cup goal for the club, which proved to be the winner in a fourth-round victory over Charlton Athletic. Very rarely did he venture upfield, but when he did he always caused a problem for opposing defenders, and, in fact, in the opening League game of the 1930–31 season versus Sheffield United, besides his goal, he also hit the woodwork and had a header kicked off the line in a 3–1 win.

Morrall added a further 43 senior appearances to his tally before he stepped down from first-team duty, handing over to the tall figure of Tom Fillingham who had been his deputy since 1932. In June 1936 he left St Andrew's for Swindon Town, where he remained until his retirement in May 1940. He was only 50 when he died in 1955. His nephew, Terry Morrall, played for Aston Villa, Shrewsbury Town, Wrexham and Southport between 1953 and 1966 and also managed Stourbridge.

Peter Murphy

Date of birth: 7 March 1922, West Hartlepool, County Durham
Died: 7 April 1975, Coventry

Blues record:
Appearances: League 245, FA Cup 24, Europe 9
Goals: League 107, FA Cup 16, Europe 4
Debut: League, 28 January 1952 v Doncaster Rovers (a) won 5–0

Also played for: Dunlop FC, Middlesbrough (trial), Millwall (guest), Coventry City, Tottenham Hotspur
Managed: Rugby Town, Coventry City (A team)

Peter 'Spud' Murphy represented Coventry Schools and was a trialist with Middlesbrough, an amateur inside-forward with both Coventry City and Birmingham City and played as a guest for Millwall during World War Two before signing professional forms at Highfield Road in May 1946.

After four excellent years with the Sky Blues, for whom he scored 37 goals in 119 appearances, Murphy was transferred to Tottenham Hotspur in June 1950 for £18,500 – a healthy sum in those days. Playing in the same forward line as Len Duquemin, Sonny Walters and England internationals Eddie Baily and Les Medley, he helped the London club win the Second Division Championship in 1951, netting nine times in 25 matches when appearing as deputy for Les Bennett. However, he became unsettled in London when a fit again Bennett and Tommy Harmer were also contesting the inside-forward positions. He subsequently left White Hart Lane for St Andrew's in a £20,000 deal in January 1952, having notched 21 goals in 49 first-team outings for Spurs.

Murphy linked up with Billy Wardle on Blues' left wing and on his debut cracked in a hat-trick in a 5–0 League win at Doncaster. He went on to strike home seven goals in the last 15 League games of that season, adding 26 (in League and Cup) to his tally in 1952–53, as Blues missed out on promotion to the top flight, finishing in sixth position. For the 1953–54 campaign, Blues manager Arthur Turner replaced Wardle with sprightly Scotsman Alex Govan, and he and Murphy began what was to be a terrific partnership down the left flank. They hit 22 goals between them that season, while in 1954–55 they bagged 36 in total, Murphy top scoring with 20, and Birmingham clinched the Second Division Championship on goal average from Luton Town thanks to a last-match victory at Doncaster 5–1 when he was among the marksmen.

In form at this juncture, the following season Murphy weighed in with another 17 goals, including five in the FA Cup as Blues went through to the Final at Wembley, where they lost to Manchester City. In fact, Peter was the unlucky player who accidentally collided with Bert Trautmann, the City goalkeeper, causing the German to fracture his neck.

Murphy's phenomenal left-foot shooting, mainly from 30 to 40 yards out, often caused problems for opposing goalkeepers and such was his marksmanship that he topped the scoring charts on four occasions during his time with Blues, having his best season in 1952–53 and his second best in 1957–58 when he notched 23 goals.

In his last two seasons at St Andrew's – 1958–59 and 1959–60 – Murphy managed only 19 starts in the first team, scoring eight times to finish with an excellent record of 127 goals in 278 first-team outings. He officially retired in the summer of 1959 when he was handed a coaching job at St Andrew's, but with Blues battling against relegation the following season he came back to help them avoid the drop, grabbing two goals in a 3–0 home win over Arsenal and two more in a 4–2 victory at Sheffield Wednesday.

A supreme marksman, Murphy ended his post-World War Two career with 185 goals to his credit in just under 450 League and Cup appearances amassed with three clubs.

In 1960–61 Murphy guided non-League outfit Rugby Town to promotion to the Southern League Premier Division and later returned to Highfield Road to manage Coventry's A team before going into the licensing trade, where he worked as a representative for Davenports Brewery.

Peter, who initially moved to the Midlands with his family at the age of four, was only 53 years of age when he died in 1975.

Bert Murray

Date of birth: 22 September 1942, Shoreditch, London

Blues record:
Appearances: League 127+9, FA Cup 12+1, League Cup 13
Goals: League 22, FA Cup 0, League Cup 1
Debut: League, 20 August 1966 v Wolverhampton Wanderers (a) 2–1

Also played for: Chelsea, Brighton & Hove Albion, Peterborough United, England (3 Youth and 6 Under-23 caps)

Taking over on the right-wing from Alec Jackson, Bert Murray made a terrific start to his career with Blues, scoring both goals on his senior debut in a 2–1 win at Midlands rivals Wolves on the opening day of the 1966–67 Second Division season. Prior to that he had done exceedingly well with Chelsea, whom he joined straight from school as an apprentice in June 1958, turning professional two years later. He switched to St Andrew's for what was to prove a bargain fee of just £25,000. He netted 44 goals in 183 senior appearances for the London club, gaining a League Cup-winners' tankard in 1965 against Leicester City and helping his side reach the semi-finals of the Inter Cities Fairs Cup a year later, while also playing in six Under-23 internationals for England, having earlier represented his country at both Schoolboy and Youth-team levels.

Nicknamed 'Ruby' – after the famous female singer – Murray occupied the right-wing position for Chelsea, but he lined up at outside-left (wearing the number-11 shirt) and also at inside and outside-right during his first three-and-a-half months with Blues before being switched to the right-back berth in place of the injured Ray Martin in December 1966. He did a wonderful job as an attacking wing-back, and in 1967–68 formed an excellent quartet down Blues' right flank with skipper Ron Wylie, his former Chelsea teammate Barry Bridges and the influential Johnny Vincent.

Murray appeared in 52 competitive games in his first season at St Andrew's (nine goals scored) and 47 in his second (two goals) but was a bitterly disappointed player when Blues lost in two Cup semi-finals in successive years, going down 7–2 on aggregate to Queen's Park Rangers in the League Cup of 1967 and 2–0 to near-neighbours West Bromwich Albion at neutral Villa Park in the FA Cup in 1968.

Unfortunately Murray was plagued by a series of niggling knee and ankle injuries during the 1968–69 campaign, managing only 11 first-team appearances. Thankfully, he regained full fitness and got back into the side for the 1969–70 season when he was switched back to his old position on the right wing, where he was accompanied this time round by a new inside partner in Trevor Hockey and had both Malcolm Beard and Malcolm Page assisting him from behind, Martin having returned to the side at right-back. Blues had a decent side at this time and were among the favourites to gain promotion to the top flight in the early 1970s, but soon after Freddie Goodwin had taken over as team manager from Stan Cullis, and Murray himself had chalked up his 160th senior appearance for the club against Huddersfield Town in a third-round FA Cup replay, he was surprisingly transferred to Brighton & Hove Albion for £10,000 in February 1971, having been replaced on the right wing at St Andrew's by Alan Campbell, as Goodwin chopped and changed his team around, formulated a different style of play and, indeed, introduced completely new tactics to those used by his predecessor.

Murray made over 100 League appearances for Brighton, whom he served until September 1973 when he switched his allegiance to Peterborough United. Four years later, having taken his career appearance record at club level to almost 600 (108 goals scored), he announced his retirement at the age of 35 but continued thereafter to play regularly in various charity matches arranged by Chelsea and Brighton. In later life he entered the pub trade and was landlord of the White Horse Inn at Market Deeping, Lincolnshire, for many years.

Dick Neal

Date of birth: 1 October 1933, Dinnington near Sheffield

Blues record:
Appearances: League 165, FA Cup 12, League Cup 4, Europe 16
Goals: League 15, FA Cup 1, League Cup 1, Europe 1
Debut: League, 23 April 1957 v West Bromwich Albion (h) won 2–0

Also played for: Dinnington Miners' Welfare, Wath Wanderers, Wolverhampton Wanderers, Middlesbrough, Lincoln City (two spells), Rugby Town, Hednesford Town (player-manager), Brierley Hill (player-manager), Blakenhall (player-manager), England (4 Under-23 caps)

Powerfully built, 6ft 1in tall, weighing 12st 10lbs and reckoned by many to be useful in most defensive positions and also as an emergency striker if required, Yorkshire-born Dick 'Ticker' Neal entered League football with Lincoln City after being unable to make much progress with the new League champions Wolverhampton Wanderers. He was signed by Imps boss Bill Anderson – on the recommendation of Stan Cullis – for £1,000 in July 1954 – this after he had failed to get into the first XI at Molineux owing to the presence and, indeed, the form, of so many quality players who were at the club at that time, including Ron Flowers, Bill Slater, Eddie Clamp and Billy Wright, all of whom either were or became full England internationals.

Neal, who learned a lot during his time with Wolves (signed initially as a junior in August 1949 and upgraded to the professional ranks in March 1951), quickly bedded himself in at Sincil Bank and went on to accumulate 115 League appearances and collected three England Under-23 caps in two years, against Denmark and France in 1956 and Scotland in 1957, before transferring to Blues for £18,500 plus forward Bert Linnecor in April 1957. He immediately added a fourth Under-23 cap to his tally against Bulgaria and also represented Young England against England in the annual challenge match.

Neal replaced Roy Warhurst in the left-half position in Blues' senior side, having an impressive debut in a 2–0 home win over West Midlands neighbours West Bromwich Albion. The following season he missed only two League games and scored four goals, his first against Burnley at Turf Moor in September 1957 (lost 3–1). He also lined up for Blues in the two-leg semi-final of the Inter Cities Fairs Cup against Barcelona, which eventually ended in defeat after a replay in Switzerland.

During seasons 1958–59 and 1959–60 Neal made almost 100 senior appearances, hardly missing a League game and helping Blues finish ninth and 19th in the First Division and reach the Final of the Fairs Cup in the latter year where they lost over two legs to the Italian club AS Roma.

The League Cup was introduced in 1960 and Neal played in Blues' first game in this competition against Bradford Park Avenue (away) which ended in a 1–0 win. He was now part of a terrific half-back line at St Andrew's, his colleagues being Johnny Watts (soon to be replaced by Terry Hennessey) and England international Trevor Smith. He went on to serve Blues honestly and professionally until October 1961 when he was transferred to Middlesbrough for £23,000. He spent just under two years at Ayresome Park, adding a further 38 senior appearances to his tally (four goals) before returning to his former club Lincoln City for £3,000 in August 1963. Taking his overall record with the Imps to 156 games and 15 goals, he decided to quit top-line competitive football in October 1964 with a total of 415 League appearances under his belt. At that point he joined Warwickshire-based Rugby Town, later having spells as player-manager with three other non-League clubs, Hednesford Town, Brierley Hill and Blakenhall (Wolverhampton).

In later in life Neal, whose father Richard senior played for Blackpool, Derby County, Southampton, Bristol City and Accrington Stanley between the two World Wars, became a licensee, first in the West Midlands and later taking over as mine host at the Horse and Jockey at Penkridge.

Vince Overson

Date of birth: 15 May 1952, Kettering, Northamptonshire

Blues record:
Appearances: League 179+3, FA Cup 8, League 11+1, others 11
Goals: League 3, FA Cup 0, League Cup 0, others 1
Debut: League, 23 August 1986 v Stoke City (a) won 2–0

Also played for: Corby Town, Long Buckby, Burnley (two spells), Stoke City, Shrewsbury Town (loan), Halifax Town, Padiham FC

Central-defender Vince Overson, who played for England at Youth-team level, made 247 senior appearances as a professional for Burnley from 1968 before joining Blues for £235,000 in June 1986 – signed by manager Garry Pendrey to bolster up his back line following relegation to the Second Division. Brought in to replace Ken Armstrong, he made his debut for the club against his future employers Stoke City in front of 11,500 hardy supporters at the Victoria Ground. He played very well in a 2–0 win and retained his place at the heart of the defence alongside Jim Hagan. However, halfway through the season he was injured in a 2–2 draw at Reading, and he played only once more during the next two months before returning in early March to help Blues pull clear of the trapdoor leading into the Third Division.

The following season Overson appeared in 37 League games and three Cup ties, and once again his outstanding efforts were greatly appreciated by all and sundry as Blues, for the second season running, escaped the drop by the skin of their teeth, finishing in 19th position, safe by just two points. However, it was to be a completely different story in 1988–89 – and this time, despite his brave and dogged performances, when he missed only five League games, Blues crashed through the trapdoor and into the Third Division for the first time in the club's history, going down with Walsall and Shrewsbury Town while being replaced by Midland neighbours Wolves, Sheffield United and Port Vale.

Obviously despondent, Overson nevertheless rolled up his sleeves, and, along with his colleagues, publicly vowed that Blues would be making a concerted effort at winning promotion at the first attempt. Unfortunately the team's overall performances were rather inconsistent, and in the end they had to settle for seventh place in the table, 21 points short of an automatic place. In fact at one stage they were in danger of being dragged into the relegation zone – and that was frightening.

It was a tough campaign but once again Overson, although disappointed, maintained that Blues were not a Third Division club and given the breaks could be a force to be reckoned with in 1990–91. It didn't happen. Blues struggled in the League both at home and away and finished a poor 12th – although they did go all the way to Wembley where they won the Leyland DAF Trophy, beating Tranmere Rovers 3–2.

At this juncture, Overson stunned everyone by walking out on Blues, joining his former manager Lou Macari at Stoke City, signed for a tribunal-fixed fee of £55,000. He had appeared in well over 200 games for Blues, his wholehearted approach making him a firm favourite with the supporters, although it must be said that his relationship with the directors and other members of the St Andrew's personnel wasn't always amicable – plus the fact that his wife didn't really settle in the West Midlands.

Overson went on to appear in 216 first-class matches for the Potters (seven goals scored), making a return trip to Wembley where he helped them win the Auto-glass Trophy against Stockport County, followed by the Second Division Championship in 1993. In August 1996 he completed a full circle by returning to his former club Burnley, later assisting Shrewsbury Town (on loan), Halifax Town and Lancashire non-League side Padiham before announcing his retirement through injury in 2000.

Overson's brother Richard played for Burnley and Hereford United.

Malcolm Page

Date of birth: 5 February 1947, Knucklas, Radnorshire, Wales

Blues record:
Appearances: League 328+11, FA Cup 29, League Cup 14, others 12
Goals: League 9, FA Cup 1, League Cup 0, others 0
Debut: League, 6 February 1965 v Everton (a) drew 1–1

Also played for: Oxford United, Wales (6 Under-23 and 28 full caps)

If you were to scrutinise in detail Malcolm Page's statistics, especially his playing record in terms of appearance and positions occupied, you would appreciate what a terrific club man he was – a wonderfully consistent and versatile footballer who was second to none when it came to effort and commitment, dedication and endeavour. While his personal preference was to play in midfield, he was unperturbed at being asked to fill in at full-back, as a central-defender, a sweeper, as an orthodox wing-half, even as a wide man, an inside-right or left or pushing forward. He simply loved his football and would play in any position just to get a game. In fact, during his time with Blues Malcolm donned every numbered jersey except the goalkeeper's. Very much a players' player, he certainly earned the respect and admiration of his fellow professionals.

Page's adaptability was first class and it was, no doubt, his versatility that proved to be a great advantage to his managers – first Gil Merrick (who signed him following a recommendation from Blues scout Don Dorman, who had seen him in action playing for Wales in one of four Schoolboy internationals), then Joe Mallett, followed by Stan Cullis, Freddie Goodwin, Willie Bell, Sir Alf Ramsey and finally Jim Smith. And talking of managers, very few players have played under seven for the same club!

Page, encouraged by his father Bill, a South Shropshire League referee, to play football instead of rugby, joined Blues soon after leaving Knighton Secondary Modern School, Radnorshire, in late May 1964. He turned professional in September of that same year, and after doing well in the reserves he made his League debut just 24 hours after his 18th birthday, in the number-eight shirt (inside-right) in front of 34,000 fans in a 1–1 draw with Everton at Goodison Park – the first of 394 senior appearances Malcolm made for Blues.

Page secured a regular place in the side during the 1967–68 campaign when Blues lost to West Bromwich Albion in the FA Cup semi-final – having made only 18 appearances in three seasons prior to that – and when fit was one of the first names his manager put on the team sheet. He made a total of 48 appearances in 1971–72 when Blues gained promotion from the Second Division as runners'-up and again slipped up in an FA Cup semi-final, losing this time to Leeds United, and he was still a key member of the side seven years later when Blues were relegated, only to return to top-flight football at the first attempt. In 1975 Page, along with his teammates, were distraught once more when for the third time he lost an FA Cup semi-final, this time to Fulham in a replay. He was also disappointed three years later when Blues slipped into the Second Division, but overall he certainly enjoyed as many highs as he did lows as a footballer.

Page gained 28 full caps for Wales – the most ever by a Blues player. His first came against Finland in Helsinki in May 1971 (three days before his wedding) and his last eight years later versus West Germany. His finest performance in his country's red shirt was against Hungary in Budapest in 1975 when he helped Wales win 2–1 on their way to the quarter-finals of the European Championship.

Lying in ninth position in the list of Blues' all-time appearance makers, Page spent almost 17 years at St Andrew's, moving to Oxford United in February 1981 and retiring in March of the following year to take up employment as an insurance company representative. Now working for a civil engineering firm near St Andrew's, he plays golf rather than attending football matches.

Garry Pendrey

Date of birth: 9 February 1949, Lozells, Birmingham

Blues record:
Appearances: League 287+19, FA Cup 15+1, League Cup 21+2, others 14+1
Goals: League 4, FA Cup 0, League Cup 1, others 0
Debut: League, 8 March 1969, as substitute v Crystal Palace (h) drew 0–0
Manager: June 1987–July 1989

Also played for: Stanley Star, Harborne Lynwood, West Bromwich Albion, Torquay United, Bristol Rovers, Walsall
Also managed: Walsall

The versatile Garry Pendrey skippered Blues' successful youth team in the late 1960s when they reached the Final of the FA Youth Cup. Later leading both the reserve and senior sides, he became the club's youngest-ever senior captain in 1969 at the age of 20 years six months, perhaps being a shade too young to appreciate the responsibility.

Able to play at left-back (his favourite position), left-half, as a sweeper or in midfield, Pendrey went on to give Blues excellent service for more than 14 years, during which time he played in 360 first-class matches, placing him 12th in the club's all-time list of top appearance makers.

After representing Aston Boys (Birmingham), Pendrey signed as an apprentice at St Andrew's in July 1965 and turned professional in October 1966. Making his debut as a substitute against Crystal Palace in March 1969, he made nine League appearances that season as a left-sided defender and followed up with 29 in 1969–70 when he had his first outing in the League Cup against Brighton. Now an established member of the side, his tenacious tackling and total commitment endeared him to the Blues' supporters, and in 1970–71 Pendrey played in 32 senior games, missing several matches through injury.

The following season, however, Pendrey was back to full fitness and in terrific form, helping Blues gain promotion to the First Division and reach the FA Cup semi-final (beaten by Leeds United). He played in 49 senior matches in 1971–72 and netted his first goal for the club, in a 3–0 home League win over Cardiff City in late December. Occasionally used in midfield by Blues manager Freddie Goodwin in 1972–73, he adapted perfectly to First Division football, producing some excellent displays against some quality footballers. He was absent from just two League games and scored a fine goal in a 4–1 home victory over Norwich City in late December.

In 1973–74 Pendrey played alongside Ray Martin at full-back and was outstanding, and was just as good in 1974–75 when he lined up at left-half as Blues again reached the FA Cup semi-finals, losing this time to Fulham after a replay in extra-time at Maine Road.

Injuries affected Pendrey's performances in 1975–76 (21 outings) and also in 1976–77 (28 games), but he was in fine form the following season when partnering Jimmy Calderwood in front of goalkeeper Jim Montgomery as Blues finished a creditable 11th in the top flight. Unfortunately 12 months later Blues were relegated, going down in 21st position, Pendrey missing most of the campaign, having lost his place in the side to Mark Dennis. He was granted a testimonial against West Bromwich Albion at the end of that season, and, perhaps surprisingly, he moved to The Hawthorns shortly after, signed by Albion manager Ron Atkinson for £30,000.

Pendrey spent two seasons with the Baggies, and after spells with Torquay United and Bristol Rovers he returned to the Midlands to become player-coach of Walsall in July 1982, later taking over as assistant manager in May 1983 to August 1986. He then came back to St Andrew's as manager in June 1987, holding office for two years and seeing Blues slip into the Third Division, before switching to Wolves as senior coach in July 1989. He stayed at Molineux for almost five years (to March 1994) and after a year out of the game returned as coach at Coventry City, initially under manager Phil Neal and later to his former boss Ron Atkinson. He was named assistant manager in November to Gordon Strachan, and he followed the former Manchester United and Scottish international to Southampton in October 2001 and Celtic in 2005. He also appeared for West Bromwich Albion Old Stars in well over 100 charity matches (1982–90).

Paul Peschisolido

Date of birth: 25 May 1971, Pickering, Scarborough, Ontario, Canada

Blues record:
Appearances: League 44+8, FA Cup 0+1, League Cup 2, others 1+1
Goals: League 17, FA Cup 0, League Cup 1, others 0
Debut: Anglo-Italian Cup, 11 November 1992 v Bari (h) won 1–0

Also played for: Toronto Blizzard (NASL, two spells), Juventus (Italy, loan), Kansas City Comets (NASL), Stoke City, West Bromwich Albion, Fulham, Queen's Park Rangers, Sheffield United (two spells), Norwich City (loan), Derby County, Canada (11 Under-23 and 51 full caps, plus 9 appearances in the Olympic Games)

Impish striker Paul Pasquale Peschisolido was associated with Blues for less than two seasons, but in that time he became a huge favourite with the fans.

Born to Italian parents who emigrated to North America in 1978, Peschisolido made rapid progress as a youngster and represented Canada in the Under-16 World Cup tournament in 1985. He later spent a disappointing season on loan with Juventus before signing for Blues for £25,000 from Toronto Blizzard in November 1992 – two years after being voted the Major Indoor Soccer League's Newcomer of the Year, while playing for Kansas City Comets.

By now a Canadian international at senior level, Peschisolido quickly made his mark at St Andrew's with his fast, enterprising runs, which carried him deep into the opposing penalty area. He netted seven times in 22 games in his first season, including the winners at home to Oxford and Sunderland and a brace in a 2–0 victory at Brentford. Linking up splendidly with Andy Saville and Paul Moulden late in the campaign, their joint efforts helped save Blues from relegation, a last-gasp home win over Charlton doing the trick.

The following season 'Pesch' was joint top scorer with Saville on 10 goals, but this time their joint contributions were in vain as Blues suffered relegation from the First Division, going down in 22nd place. At that point, although reluctant to leave, he was transferred to Stoke City for £400,000 in a player-exchange deal involving David Regis.

Peschisolido did well with the Potters, netting 24 goals in 81 outings before moving back to Blues for the same figure (£400,000) in July 1996. He stayed at St Andrew's for only four months, adding one more goal to his tally in nine games. He was then sold to neighbours West Bromwich Albion for £600,000, and at The Hawthorns, like he had been with Blues, he became a cult hero with the supporters. He hit 21 goals for the Baggies, including two hat-tricks, one as a substitute versus Bury, in 51 appearances before moving to Fulham for £1.1 million in October 1997, shortly before he was named Canada's Player of the Year. He was also named Cottager's Player of the Year for 1999 after the London club's successful promotion campaign from the Second to First Division under manager Kevin Keegan. However, after Keegan was replaced by Paul Bracewell, 'Pesch' lost his way and eventually left as well, joining Sheffield United for £150,000 in July 2001, having previously been on loan at Bramall Lane and also at Queen's Park Rangers and Norwich.

After some fine performances for the Blades, for whom 'Pesch' struck 22 goals in almost 100 games, helping them reach the semi-finals of both the League and FA Cup competitions and the Play-off Final against Wolves in the First Division at the Millennium Stadium, which they lost, he was signed by Derby County in March 2004. Two years later he was a loser again in the Play-offs, this time in the semi-final.

Peschisolido has now netted well over 160 goals in 645 appearances in club and international football. His international career spanned 13 and a half years, and he made the first of his 51 senior appearances for Canada against Hong Kong in 1992 and his last in 2005 when his country failed to qualify for the World Cup Finals in Germany. He netted 10 goals in total. In all, he appeared against 25 different countries, and was sent off and subsequently suspended after being dismissed during the final round of qualifying matches in the lead up to France '98. His red card came against El Salvador and was completely unwarranted. Upset at being fouled, he flipped the corner flag into the face of an El Salvador defender, who went down like a ton of bricks. FIFA later added to the automatic one-game suspension.

Peschisolido is married to current Blues managing director Karen Brady and the couple have two children.

Fred Pickering

Date of birth: 19 January 1941, Blackburn

Blues record:
Appearances: League 42, FA Cup 11, League Cup 3
Goals: League 13, FA Cup 5, League Cup 0
Debut: League, 19 August 1967 v Bolton Wanderers (h) won 4–0

Also played for: Blackburn Rovers (two spells), Everton, Blackpool, Brighton & Hove Albion (trial), England (3 Under-23 and 3 full caps)

An FA Youth Cup winner with Blackburn Rovers in 1959, centre-forward Fred Pickering had an excellent first spell at Ewood Park, scoring 72 goals in a total of 146 senior appearances over a period of five years, during which time he also gained three England Under-23 caps against Wales and West Germany in 1963 and Scotland in 1964.

Originally a rather ordinary left-back, Pickering's career underwent a complete metamorphosis when he was selected, as a gamble, to lead the Rovers attack by manager Jack Marshall in March 1961 against Manchester City, scoring twice in a 3–1 win. He never looked back after that, and following his £85,000 transfer to the reigning League champions Everton in March 1964, which clearly annoyed the Rovers fans, he celebrated his arrival at Merseyside with a splendid hat-trick on his debut as Nottingham Forest were beaten 6–1.

Two months later a confident Pickering bagged another treble on his full international baptism in an emphatic 10–0 win over the USA in New York, when Liverpool's Roger Hunt (4 goals), Southampton's Terry Paine (2) and Manchester United's Bobby Charlton (1) along with some brilliant midfield wing play by Peter Thompson (also from Liverpool) battered the American defence.

Disappointingly Pickering played only twice more for his country at senior level, scoring in both games in a 4–3 win over Northern Ireland in Belfast five months later and in a 2–2 draw with Belgium at Wembley a fortnight after that. He also represented the Football League as an Everton player. Owing to injury, he missed Everton's 1966 FA Cup Final win over Sheffield Wednesday, replaced in attack by Mike Trebilcock, and following the emergence of a young Joe Royle, he moved to Birmingham in August 1967 for £50,000, having netted 70 goals in 115 games for Everton – a brilliant return.

Pickering was strong and mobile, fast over the ground with good skills and heading ability, and he slotted into the Blues attack a treat, linking up superbly with Barry Bridges to his right and Geoff Vowden to his left. An ever present, he netted 15 goals in his first season at St Andrew's, helping Blues finish fourth in Division Two and reach the FA Cup semi-finals, where they lost 2–0 to West Bromwich Albion. In fact, he was brilliant that afternoon and only the Baggies' goalkeeper John Osborne stood between him and a hat-trick. He struck his first goal in a Blues shirt in a 6–2 home win over Hull City and later netted twice in a 6–1 thumping of Huddersfield Town, also at St Andrew's, 48 hours before Christmas. He also notched a beauty against Chelsea in an FA Cup tie at St Andrew's in front of 51,576 fans, which took Blues into the semi-finals for the first time since 1957.

Joint top scorer with Phil Summerill with 17 goals in the 1968–69 campaign – a haul that included three braces – in home wins over Portsmouth (5–2) and Bristol City (2–0) and in a 3–2 defeat at his former club Blackburn – Pickering had a few injury problems during the early autumn but battled on before being deemed surplus to requirements by Blues manager Stan Cullis, who allowed to him leave after a lengthy discussion for pastures new in June 1969, Pickering agreeing to join First Division Blackpool for a fee of £45,000. He helped the Seasiders win promotion and later returned for a second spell at Ewood Park (signed for £5,000 in March 1971), and he also had an unsuccessful trial at Brighton & Hove Albion (from February 1972) before announcing his retirement from first-class football, basically through injury, in May 1972, at the age of 32.

Later in life, when he put on a lot of weight, Pickering was employed as a fork-lift truck driver for a plastics firm near his native Blackburn.

Ray Ranson

Date of birth: 12 June 1960, St Helens, Lancashire

Blues record:
Appearances: League 136+1, FA Cup 10, League Cup 9, others 2
Goals: 0
Debut: League, 17 November 1984 v Charlton Athletic (a) lost 2–1

Also played for: Manchester City (two spells), Newcastle United, Reading, Witton Albion (player-manager), England (9
                 Schoolboy, 6 Youth and 10 Under-21 caps)

Ray Ranson was an attacking right-back (one of the early wing-backs) who possessed good speed, neat ball control and had the ability to put over pin-point crosses. He was useful at defending, too, and was often in the right place at the right time to clear the danger, often kicking the ball off the line when his goalkeeper was beaten.

After signing for Manchester City as an apprentice in June 1976, turning professional in June 1977, Ranson gained a regular place in the first XI at Maine Road while still in his teens and quickly progressed to the England Under-21s, skippering the team on several occasions while gaining a total of 10 caps in 1981 and 1982, having earlier represented his country at both Schoolboy and Youth-team levels.

After making well over 200 senior appearances for City and collecting an FA Cup runners'-up medal in 1981 (beaten in a replay by Tottenham Hotspur), Ranson had a disagreement with the club after being relegated to the junior team by new manager Billy McNeill. With his career at a crossroads, he went on the transfer list and was subsequently transferred to Blues for a fee of £15,000 in November 1984, signed by ex-Manchester City boss Ron Saunders.

Ranson went straight into the team at right-back, allowing Brian Roberts to switch over to the opposite flank. He made a moderate debut in a 2–1 League defeat at Charlton but after that produced some excellent displays, helping Blues win promotion from the Second Division as runners-up to Oxford United, missing the title by just two points. He made 32 appearances in 1984–85 and 41 the following campaign which, sadly, wasn't a good one all round for Blues, who were relegated back to the Second Division, going down in 21st place.

Injuries affected Ranson's form in 1986–87, and he played in only 21 senior matches, Mark Jones, Brian Roberts, Tommy Williams and Kevin Ashley all deputising for him at full-back. He regained full fitness for the 1987–88 season when he played alongside Julian Dicks, but he was in a struggling team as Blues scrambled clear of relegation, claiming 19th place in the table. Things weren't right at St Andrew's – not helped by three changes of manager in double-quick time – but he stuck in there and started the next season playing, once more, as partner to Brian Roberts. Blues continued to struggle and with the team bottom of the ladder and heading to the Third Division, he moved on to pastures new, joining Newcastle United for £175,000 in December 1988.

Recruited by ex-Blues manager Jim Smith, it was hoped that Ranson would bring experience and a certain amount of guile to the Geordies' defence, but he found it difficult to settle in at St James' Park. However, with some accomplished performances he gradually won over the fans, some of whom had been rather hasty in their criticisms of him. But after making just over 100 senior appearances in the black and white stripes, injury rocked his progress, and he found himself in the treatment room with pelvic and Achilles tendon problems.

Ranson missed over a year of action, and by the time he was back to full training Kevin Keegan was manager and there was a new batch of Magpies in vogue. This was a cue for his rather topsy-turvy career to take another turn. After a loan spell back at Maine Road, he left Newcastle for Reading in August 1993, helping the Royals win the Second Division title at the end of his first season. He remained at Elm Park until the summer of 1995 when he entered non-League football as player-manager of Witton Albion.

On retiring in May 1997, Ranson became a partner in a well-established insurance business, based in Manchester. He did well and is now a self-made millionaire. His company was willing to buy out Aston Villa Football Club for a reported £45m but Chairman Doug Ellis said 'no way', and in the early 2000s he also showed an interest in his former club Manchester City, seeking to become a director.

'Harry' Roberts

Date of birth: 6 November 1955, Manchester

Blues record:
Appearances: League 182+5, FA Cup 9, League Cup 14+1, others 1+1
Goals: 0
Debut: League, 17 March 1984 v Stoke City (a) lost 2–1

Also played for: Coventry City, Hereford United (loan), Wolverhampton Wanderers

Harry Roberts was actually christened Brian, but during his early days with Coventry City he was given the nickname 'Harry' after a notorious gangster and train robber from the 1960s.

During his early days at Highfield Road, Roberts was regarded as 'Mr Dependable' and played in several positions, including right and left-back, wide midfield and centre-forward! Strangely, his first 10 senior appearances for the Sky Blues were all away from home, including one against Birmingham City in March 1978. In this period he also had a loan spell with Hereford United (February 1975). He finally gained a regular place in the Coventry side in August 1980 when Bobby McDonald left the club. He bedded himself in superbly well at right-back, later switching to the left when Danny Thomas moved on, and hardly missed a game until his departure to Blues for what was regarded as a paltry £10,000 in March 1984 – secured via the club's 'Buy a Player Fund' organised by supporters. He returned to Highfield Road for a deserved testimonial six months later.

A frustrating player at times, Roberts, who sometimes didn't look good enough to figure in the First Division, made 249 senior appearances for Coventry, scoring two goals, his first coming in December 1982 at West Ham, his 160th match. To celebrate the occasion, some supporters had special badges designed, stating 'I saw Harry score a goal.'

Possessing a big heart and a good turn of speed, it is fair to say that Harry had six traumatic years as a player at St Andrew's, twice asking for a transfer! He suffered relegation for the first time in his career at the end of his first season (1984), helped Blues win promotion in 1985 (as runners-up), went back down again with them in 1986, struggled desperately for survival at the foot of Division Two in both 1987 and 1988, crashed through the trapdoor into the Third Division in 1989 and finished seventh in that section in 1990.

A cheerful, likeable chap with a great sense of humour who had to work hard to win over the boo-boys at St Andrew's, Roberts played in 213 senior games for Blues (only seven as a substitute), having his best seasons in terms of appearances in 1984–85 when he played 49 times, followed by 46 outings in his last season in 1989–90. He had several full-back partners during his association with Blues, including Jim Hagan, Pat Van den Hauwe, Mark Jones, Ray Ranson and Julian Dicks, and when he was switched to a different position, especially at the heart of the defence, he played alongside 10 different players, never really having a regular partner. But he never moaned, never grumbled, he just got on with the game he loved, that of playing football.

When Roberts joined Wolves in June 1990 on a free transfer, he became a cult hero at Molineux and passed the personal milestone of 500 club appearances while with the Black County club. On retiring in July 1992 he returned to Coventry as a senior scout before taking over as reserve-team coach. He was also employed on a part-time basis as a soccer coach at Knightlow School, Stretton-on-Dunsmore, near Coventry.

In later years Harry scribed a witty column in a local Saturday night sports paper and also wrote a book called *Harry's Game*.

Arthur Robinson

Date of birth:	28 February 1878, Coventry
Died:	15 May 1929, Coventry

Blues record:

Appearances:	League 283, FA Cup 23
Goals:	0
Debut:	League, 2 September 1899 v Walsall (h) won 3–2

Also played for: Allesley FC, Coventry Stars, Singers FC, Chelsea, Coventry City

Known to all and sundry as 'Nat' Robinson, this tall, competent and sometimes eccentric goalkeeper used to jump up and down on his line, swirling his arms around like Catherine wheels to put opponents off. He also loved to race out of his area and fly-kick the ball to safety, and was often heard whistling when a corner-kick was about to be taken. He served Blues for 10 years, making over 300 appearances. He was all set to join his home-town club, Coventry City, before Blues stepped in and secured his services as a professional in August 1898. He understudied Harry Clutterbuck for a season before taking over the number-one position at the start of the 1899–1900 campaign. He had a very good first season in the side, being an ever present and conceding only 38 League goals as Blues finished an agonising third behind promoted Sheffield Wednesday and Bolton Wanderers at the top of the Second Division.

The following season, when he missed only one game at New Brighton, Robinson was outstanding, helping Blues clinch second spot in the table and secure their place in the top flight. He kept 14 clean sheets in League action and two more in the FA Cup. An ever present again in 1901–02, when, disappointingly, Blues were relegated after spending just one season with the big boys, he missed five matches through injury and illness the following term when normal service was restored as Blues once again achieved promotion.

One of the fittest players at the club, Robinson used to train for hours on his own, and he was absent from the opening three matches in 1903–04 when Blues conceded 10 goals! Consistency was certainly the main feature of his game as far as he was concerned, and from 12 September 1903 through to 6 October 1906, he played in 121 consecutive first-class games for Blues.

Robinson was quite brilliant in home games against Sheffield United and Derby County in 1904–05, versus Aston Villa, Stoke, Liverpool and Everton the following season and against Bristol City, away, and both Middlesbrough and Sheffield United at home in 1906–07. If it hadn't been for the form of other 'keepers during this period, one feels that he may well have played for England. All he had to show for his efforts was a couple of outings for the Football League against the Irish and Scottish Leagues in 1906–07 and two international trails.

Injuries started to catch up with Robinson in 1907–08 (he had 14 outings only this term), and after being replaced between the posts by Jack Dorrington he moved to Chelsea in July 1908. He made only three senior appearances in two years at Stamford Bridge before joining his boyhood heroes Coventry City in May 1910, eventually announcing his retirement in April 1911 when he became licensee of the Red Lion Inn in Barrass Green, Coventry.

Robinson's total of 306 senior games for Blues puts him in the top 20 of the club's all-time appearance makers, and only three other goalkeepers have played in more first-class games, these being Gil Merrick, Harry Hibbs and Dan Tremelling – all England internationals.

Robinson, who always donned two jerseys despite the weather conditions (be it hot, cold or mixed), is also believed to have owned just two pairs of boots throughout his lengthy professional playing career. When he was registered with Chelsea, one of his boots flew off his right foot when he was taking a goal-kick. He also owned a dog named 'Ninety', so called after the number of minutes in a game.

Johnny Schofield

Date of birth: 8 February 1931, Atherstone, Warwickshire

Blues record:
Appearances: League 212, FA Cup 4, League Cup 9, Europe 12
Goals: 0
Debut: League, 4 October 1952 v Bury (a) lost 3–0

Also played for: Nuneaton Borough reserves, Wrexham, Atherstone Town (player-manager), Bromsgrove Rovers, Tamworth
Managed: Atherstone Town (second spell)

Goalkeeper Johnny Schofield was associated with Blues for 16 years. He signed professional forms for the club in February 1950, after spending a couple of seasons playing reserve-team football with Nuneaton Borough, and left St Andrew's for Wrexham in July 1966, having appeared in 237 League and Cup games.

Stout-hearted, brave and very competent, Schofield acted as understudy to England international Gil Merrick for many years before finally establishing himself in the senior team in 1959 – nine years after first setting foot inside St Andrew's. That was a long wait, but it was well worth the effort in the end. In between times, he had played exceedingly well in the Blues' second XI in the Football Combination, and he appeared in only 56 first-class games before taking over the number-one spot on a regular basis at the start of the 1959–60 season.

Schofield made his League debut in early October 1952 in a Second Division game at Bury – when Merrick was away on international duty versus Northern Ireland. His second outing followed a month later when once again Merrick was called up by England, and this was also the case the following season: Merrick out, Johnny in. Thereafter, it was only injuries that enabled Johnny to get into the team, and he made the most of his opportunities by producing some fine displays, helping Blues win the Second Division Championship in 1955 when he played in 15 games.

Schofield was called up for first-team action just four times in 1955–56 and twice the following season. He was in hospital after surviving a pit explosion at Baddesley Colliery, Tamworth, in November 1957 and from his hospital bed, and rather shaken up, he admitted that he was 'bloody lucky to be alive'. Regaining full heath and fitness, he was handed 14 senior outings in 1957–58 and 10 more in 1958–59, by which time Merrick was ready to retire.

Installed as the number-one 'keeper in August 1959, Schofield missed only two games during that campaign and appeared in 18 the following season before he was hospitalised again after fracturing his skull during the home League game against Manchester United in November 1960, when he bravely dived at the feet of centre-forward Alex Dawson. Replaced between the posts by Colin Withers, he had to wait until September 1961 before regaining his first-team place, and the following season he celebrated with his colleagues when Blues beat Aston Villa in the two-leg League Cup Final – the first major trophy success in the club's history.

Hard pressed now by Withers for regular first-team action, Schofield remained loyal to the club, and in 1964–65 he regained the number-one spot, making 38 appearances to take his tally past the 200 mark in a Blues jersey. However, following the arrival at the club of Scotsman Jim Herriot, he added just eight more senior appearances to his tally in 1965–66 before leaving St Andrew's for the Racecourse Ground. He spent two seasons with Wrexham, for whom he made 62 appearances, 52 in the Fourth Division. In August 1968 he was appointed player-manager of his home-town club Atherstone Town, and after assisting both Bromsgrove Rovers (season 1969–70) and Tamworth (for two seasons from August 1970) as a player he returned for a second spell in charge of Atherstone Town, holding office from July 1972 to May 1974. He later became the proprietor of a wines and spirits off-licence business in Atherstone, as well as being a long-standing season-ticket holder at St Andrew's.

Johnny Schofield was a truly great guy who loved his football.

Jim Smith

Date of birth: 17 October 1940, Sheffield

Blues record:
Manager: March 1978–February 1982

Played for: Sheffield United, Aldershot, Halifax Town, Lincoln City, Boston United (player-manager), Colchester United (player-manager)

Also managed: Blackburn Rovers, Oxford United (two spells), Queen's Park Rangers, Newcastle United, Portsmouth, Derby County, Southampton (assistant)

Affectionately known as 'Bald Eagle', Jim Smith is a typical tough Yorkshireman who, to a certain extent, tasted some success with virtually every club he managed. An extrovert character, he has always been very popular with the media, his outspoken views encouraging great debate in the local and national press as well as on various radio and TV channels. His greatest achievement as a manager was to steer the then unfashionable Oxford United to successive Division titles, winning the Third in 1984 and the Second in 1985. This double enabled the Manor Ground club to clinch promotion to the top flight of English football for the first time in their history.

A year later Smith led Queen's Park Rangers out at Wembley to contest the League Cup Final, against his former club Oxford. Unfortunately he had to settle for a runners'-up prize as the Londoners went down 3–0. Twelve years earlier, in 1974, he had successfully lifted Colchester United out of the Fourth Division, and in 1980 he was the hero of St Andrew's after steering Blues back into the top flight as Second Division runners-up.

Following a decent spell in charge of Blackburn Rovers, Smith took over as manager of Blues in March 1978, succeeding Sir Alf Ramsey. There's no doubt that he had a chequered four-year spell in the St Andrew's hot seat. Blues went down at the end of the 1978–79 season, but as previously stated they bounced straight back up with a pretty useful team that included several experienced players, among them Alan Curbishley, Colin Todd, the nomadic Frank Worthington, Terry Lees, Don Givens, Scottish World Cup star Archie Gemmill, Tony Evans, winger Willie Johnston and goalkeeper Jeff Wealands. The previous season he had recruited Argentinian World Cup winner Alberto Tarantini and the Walsall striker Alan Buckley for the club, neither of whom really fitted the bill. However, Smith had not tasted First Division football prior to his appointment by Blues, and he did a pretty good job as they finished 13th in the table in 1980–81. He then went out and signed two Dutch players – Bud Brocken and winger Tony van Mierlo. Results out on the pitch though were poor, and after a dismal run when only two wins were recorded in 14 games Smith was sacked, Blues' chairman Clifford Coombes saying 'The decision to terminate Jim's contract was taken purely and simply because it was felt that poor results over a fairly lengthy period of time demanded that particular course of action.'

Smith was out of the game for only a few months after leaving St Andrew's before taking over the reins at Oxford United (July 1982). He switched to QPR in June 1985, and in April of the following year he set a new football record by becoming the first man to visit all 92 League grounds as a manager for a competitive match.

To a certain extent Jim then revived the flagging fortunes of Newcastle United, whom he managed from December 1988 to March 1991, and thereafter he held the positions of either coach, assistant manager or manager at Derby County, Middlesbrough (where he worked under Colin Todd), Coventry City and Portsmouth, guiding the latter to the FA Cup semi-finals and narrowly missing promotion to the Premiership, losing to Leicester City in the Play-offs. He is currently manager for the second time at Oxford United.

Prior to his managerial career, Smith had played all his League football in the Fourth Division, pulling out in 1969 after making almost 250 senior appearances. His first triumph as a manager was to guide Boston United to victory in the Eastern Professional Floodlit Cup Final in 1972.

Trevor Smith

Date of birth: 13 April 1936, Brierley Hill, West Midlands
Died: 9 August 2003, Dagenham, Essex

Blues record:
Appearances: League 365, FA Cup 35, League Cup 12, Europe 18
Goals: League 3, FA Cup 0, League Cup 0, Europe 0
Debut: League, 31 October 1953 v Derby County (a) won 4–2

Also played for: Walsall, England (2 B, 15 Under-23 and 2 full caps)
Managed: Mile Oak Rovers

As a teenager at Quarry Bank Secondary Modern School, Trevor Smith occupied a defensive position in the Brierley Hill & Sedgley Boys side that claimed the runners'-up prize in the English Schools Trophy Final. He also appeared in a number of trial matches with Dudley Schools when lined up with and against Duncan Edwards, soon to become a superstar with Manchester United. But football-mad Smith worked hard at his game, improved his physique in the gymnasium and quickly developed into a muscular centre-half with Birmingham City, whom he served supremely well for 13 years, initially as an amateur before turning professional at the age of 17. In fact, he made his senior Blues debut (in place of the injured Jack Badham) just six months after becoming a full-time player, but he had the misfortune of conceding an own-goal, which thankfully didn't prove costly as Blues went on to register a 4–2 victory in an away Second Division fixture at Derby.

Weighing 13½st, Smith proved to be a colossus at the heart of the Blues defence. He helped the team win the Second Division Championship in 1955 (making 24 League appearances) and the following season starred in a memorable FA Cup run which took Blues through to the Final, where they lost 3–1 to Manchester City. Leading by example, he skippered the team on several occasions, including the club's appearance in the 1960 Fairs Cup Final against Barcelona, which Blues lost 4–1 on aggregate, having put on an excellent display in the first leg at St Andrew's, which ended goalless. He also skippered the team to League Cup glory in 1963 when arch-rivals Aston Villa were accounted for by 3–1, again over two legs.

In 1959, when Billy Wright announced his retirement, it was widely thought that Smith would take over the centre-half position in the England team. He played in two full internationals in a fortnight in October 1959, in a 1–1 draw with Wales at Ninian Park, Cardiff, and in the 3–2 defeat by Sweden at Wembley, but in the end manager Walter Winterbottom, after selecting Ken Brown and Peter Swan in the next two games, decided in the end to go with Peter Swan, who held the centre-half position until 1962, much to Smith's disappointment. Perhaps if he had been with a more fashionable club than Blues then he might well have made the number-five berth his own on the international front. We shall never know.

Besides those two senior caps, Smith gained 15 more at Under-23 level (between 1954 and 1959, playing against Scotland four times). He also appeared in two B internationals (1954–57), twice represented the Football League versus Irish League in the late 1950s, starred in Youth and Schoolboy internationals and played twice for the Army during his national service.

After suffering an injury during the early part of the 1964–65 season, Smith was replaced at the heart of the Birmingham defence by Winston Foster. In October 1964 he joined Walsall for £18,000, but Blues were called cheats for selling an injured player, because the unfortunate Smith only appeared in 13 matches for the Saddlers before retiring from first-class football in February 1966. He became a player in the Lichfield Sunday League (1967–68) and also managed non-League side Mile Oak Rovers for a short time (1970–71) before concentrating on his full-time employment as a manager with Thresher's Wine Stores, first in the Bull Ring (Birmingham) and then in Essex.

Jackie Stewart

Date of birth: 4 September 1921, Lochgelly, Fife, Scotland
Died: Summer 1990, Cowdenbeath, Scotland

Blues record:
Appearances: League 203, FA Cup 15
Goals: League 54, FA Cup 3
Debut: League, 17 January 1948 v Luton Town (a) won 1–0

Also played for: Lochgelly Welfare, Donbristle Youth Club, Raith Rovers (two spells)

Jackie Stewart was a fast raiding right-wing with plenty of skill, clever at getting into a good position before receiving the ball and he also possessed a cracking shot. Signed by manager Harry Storer to replace Jack Goodwin on the right flank, he became a firm favourite with the fans at St Andrew's and averaged a goal every four games for Blues, whom he served for six years before moving back to Scotland. A real bag of tricks who stood only 5ft 5ins tall and had a broad Scottish accent, he played a lot of junior football north of the border before joining Raith Rovers as a professional just prior to World War Two. During the hostilities he continued to serve the Scottish club whenever possible and did well when competitive League football resumed in the mid-1940s, being talked of in some quarters as a possibility for international honours, so much so that several scouts from many of the big-named clubs in Scotland and England went along to watch him, Blues beating them all to his signature in the end.

A former miner, Stewart made his senior debut early in 1948 at Luton, scored his first two goals in a 4–0 home win over Midlands rivals West Bromwich Albion in late March and ended the season with a Second Division Championship medal in his hand after netting seven times in 17 games, including the winner at Bradford at a crucial stage in the campaign. In September 1948 he rattled in all his side's goals when Manchester City were beaten 4–1 in a League game at St Andrew's – becoming the first winger to achieve a four-goal feat for Blues since Frank White did the trick against Brentford in December 1938. He struck home 11 goals in 37 games that season and followed up with four more in 31 starts in 1949–50, his efforts proving irrelevant, however, as Blues were relegated back to the Second Division in bottom place.

At this juncture, Johnny Berry was threatening to oust Stewart from the right-wing position, and new manager Bob Brocklebank actually started the 1950–51 campaign with Berry in the team. After just three games, Berry was switched to the left flank and Jackie re-introduced on the right as Blues set about regaining their top-flight status. They battled hard and long throughout the campaign, Stewart doing his bit with nine goals in 25 League outings, adding three more to his tally in six FA Cup ties as Blues, who claimed fourth place in the Second Division, reached the semi-final stage of the competition, only to lose 2–1 to Blackpool in a replay at Goodison Park. He weighed in with nine more goals in 1951–52, when third spot was achieved in the League, and five the following season, when at times he was sidelined through injury, a twisted knee causing most concern.

Back to full fitness at the start of 1953–54, Stewart started well enough but then lost his form, and after Gordon Astall had been recruited from Plymouth Argyle in mid-October he knew he had a fight on his hands to hold on to the right-wing position. Unfortunately, despite some enterprising displays late on in that season when he also figured at inside-right, he found himself in the reserves and made only one more senior appearance for Blues (against Leeds United at Elland Road in October 1954) before transferring back to his former club Raith Rovers in February 1955. He remained at Stark's Park until 1963, having taken over as trainer following his enforced retirement as a player in 1960. He remained in Scotland and later went into business in Cowdenbeath.

Jackie Stewart, master winger and the the fans' favourite, died in 1990, aged 69.

Lewis Stoker

Date of birth: 31 March 1911, Wheatley Hill, County Durham
Died: 17 May 1979, Birmingham

Blues record:
Appearances: League 230, FA Cup 16
Goals: League 2, FA Cup 0
Debut: League, 6 December 1930 v Huddersfield Town (h) won 2–0

Also played for: Brandon Juniors, Esh Winning Juniors, Bear Park (Durham), West Stanley, Nottingham Forest, England (3 full caps)

Lew Stoker's pen-picture in match-day programmes of the time described him as being 'a right-half of effectiveness and no little skill in tackling. His fine distribution gives splendid service to the attack.' He was certainly a fine player, confident on the ball, strong and powerful in his approach and a terrific athlete, who covered acres of ground every game.

After leaving school at the age of 14 in the summer of 1925, Stoker played junior football in and around his home county of Durham before having a month's trial with Blues in June 1930. His displays impressed manager Leslie Knighton, who signed him as a full-time professional three months later. His game developed quickly at St Andrew's, and after a dozen or so outings in the second XI he made his Football League debut in the December against Huddersfield Town, when he was brought into the side at the last minute after Alec Leslie had cried off injured. He did very well in the 2–0 win, helping set up one of the goals for Joe Bradford, and as a result he played in the next game away to Sheffield Wednesday. Unfortunately he and the rest of his colleagues had a nightmare afternoon at Hillsborough, as the Owls ran Blues ragged, winning 9–1. He appeared in five more League games that season but was overlooked for the FA Cup Final. Named as a travelling reserve, he had to sit and suffer in the stand as his teammates went down 2–1 to near neighbours West Bromwich Albion at a rain-soaked Wembley.

The following season a determined Stoker made the right-half position his own, taking over the mantle from Jimmy Cringan. He played in 41 senior matches, helping Blues finish ninth in the First Division table, the club's highest placing since 1925. A player who loved to drive forward from midfield in support of his front men, when possible he would let fly with a pile-driver from distance, although his goal return was rather disappointing. In fact, his first goal for the club came in his 169th outing, which was against Leicester City at Filbert Street in March 1935. His second followed eight months later in a 2–1 home win over Brentford.

For six years, from August 1931 to December 1937, Stoker was one of Blues' most consistent and reliable performers. In that time he appeared in 224 out of a possible 248 League and FA Cup games, only England duties preventing him from being an ever present.

In November 1932, having been on the brink of selection for quite some time, Stoker gained the first of his three full caps for England, lining up against Wales at Wrexham in a 0–0 draw. His other two international appearances for his country were against Scotland at Wembley in April 1934, when he starred in a 3–0 win, and versus Hungary in Budapest the following month, which ended in a 2–1 defeat. He also represented the Football League against the Irish League in 1932–33 and played twice for The Rest versus England and once for the Possibles versus the Probables in three international trials in the early 1930s.

Stoker went on to appear in almost 250 competitive games for Blues, having his final outing against Arsenal at Highbury in April 1938. On leaving St Andrew's he signed for Nottingham Forest, for whom he played during the first part of World War Two before retiring in 1944. Later he worked as a charge-hand at Wimbush's bakery, just a short walk from St Andrew's. His younger brother Bob played for Bolton Wanderers and Huddersfield Town during the 1930s.

Harry Storer

Date of birth: 2 February 1898, West Derby, Liverpool
Died: 1 September 1967, Derby

Blues record:
Manager: June 1945 to November 1948

Played for: Heanor Wesleyans, Marehay FC, Codnor Park FC, Riddings St James, Eastwood Bible Class, Ripley Town, Eastwood Town, Notts County (amateur), Grimsby Town, Derby County, Burnley, England (2 full caps)
Also managed: Coventry City (two spells), Derby County

Harry Storer didn't win many honours as a manager, but he was still a very good boss who, surprisingly, was never in charge of a top-class English club despite his credentials. A no-nonsense, forthright character who had no time at all for players who didn't pull their weight, Harry was hard, firm and aggressive but players under his control always knew where they stood with him. He called a spade a spade and woe-betide anyone who disobeyed his orders! Some players couldn't stand him but many others did not mind his bullying, domineering style. Quite a few, in fact, found him to be very knowledgeable about soccer and also very fair and honest with an inborn sense of humour.

Blunt, often to the point of rudeness at times, Storer had the tendency to frighten the living daylights out of some players when he first met them, and, even today, a few who knew him personally still remember the sharp-tongued football man with a heart of gold who was regarded by the late Brian Clough as the 'greatest teacher of the game.'

Stories about Storer are legendary. Once Sheffield United boss Joe Mercer complained that at least five Derby players were 'clogging.' Harry asked for their names and then Mercer inquired 'Are you going to discipline them?' 'No' replied Harry, 'I'm going to give the other six a rollicking for not trying hard enough.'

Storer came from a sporting family: his father kept goal for Woolwich Arsenal and Liverpool as well as playing cricket for Derbyshire, while his Uncle Bill played for Derby County and also cricket for Derbyshire and England. Storer himself also assisted Derbyshire as a cricketer between 1920 and 1936. He scored 13,513 runs, including 18 centuries, at an average of 27.63, and took over 200 wickets, gaining a County Championship-winners' medal in his last season. He played local football in Derbyshire and Nottinghamshire before joining Notts County at the age of 20. After World War One he signed for Grimsby Town, and as a hard tackling half-back who could also play inside-forward he scored 20 goals in 68 appearances for the Mariners before moving to Derby County for £4,500 in March 1921. He won two full England caps during his time with The Rams, lining up against France in Paris in 1924, scoring once in a 2–1 win and against Ireland in Belfast three years later. He played in 274 games for Derby, netting 63 goals, before transferring to Burnley for £4,250 in February 1929. He retired in May 1931 with a record of 88 goals in 396 club appearances to his name.

When 33 years old, Storer took his first managerial job with Coventry City in June 1931, leading the club to the Third Division South title in 1936. Many were surprised when he left Highfield Road to take charge of Blues in the summer of 1945, but his tactical knowledge and astuteness transformed the team, and in his first season at St Andrew's Blues won the Football League South title and reached the semi-finals of the FA Cup, beaten by his former club Derby County in a replay. He assembled a superb defence and two years later Blues won the Second Division Championship, conceding only 24 goals in 42 matches. He introduced some fine players as Blues manager, including Johnny Berry, Ken Green, Jackie Stewart and Martin McDonnell. In fact, he signed the latter three times – for Blues in May 1947, for Coventry in October 1949 and for Derby in July 1955.

In November 1948 Storer returned to Coventry, saying how greatly he had missed the club! Four years later the Sky Blues were relegated and after recovering from illness he was sacked in December 1953. Out of the game for 18 months, he returned to take charge of a struggling Derby County side in June 1955. He sorted things out and in 1957 they won the Third Division North title, reducing the club's overdraft from £60,000 to £23,000 by the time he left The Baseball Ground in May 1962. Later on he did some scouting for Everton.

Robin Stubbs

Date of birth: 22 April 1941, Quinton, Birmingham

Blues record:
Appearances: League 61, FA Cup 1, League Cup 5, Europe 4
Goals: League 17, FA Cup 0, League Cup 1, Europe 2
Debut: League, 28 February 1959 v West Ham United (h) won 3–0

Also played for: Torquay United (two spells), Bristol Rovers

Centre-forward Robin Stubbs was a wonderfully consistent marksman whose career brought him 185 goals in a total of 426 appearances, accumulated with three different League clubs: Blues, Torquay United and Bristol Rovers. He also weighed in with over 100 goals in various other matches, including reserve-team football. Tall, blond and rather on the slim side for a striker, he nevertheless had a great touch in front of goal, and perhaps Blues should never have let him leave St Andrew's.

A pupil at Castle Road Primary and Oldbury Grammar Schools, Stubbs represented Oldbury & District Boys before joining Blues as a 15-year-old amateur in June 1956, turning professional in April 1958 after producing some impressive displays in the youth team. Biding his time in the second XI, he finally got the nod to make his League debut from manager Arthur Beasley in February 1959 when he replaced Bryan Orritt as leader of the Blues attack for the home game with West Ham United. He did well, held his position and appeared in 11 more games that season, plus two outings in the Inter-Cities Fairs Cup competition. He scored nine League goals, including a brace in his second outing in a 7–1 win at Nottingham Forest and a hat-trick in his fourth game, which resulted in a 4–2 victory at Leicester. He was flying at this stage, and he continued to produce the goods at the start of the 1959–60 campaign, netting in a 4–3 home win over Newcastle United, a 3–2 defeat at Preston and grabbing another in a 2–0 triumph at the City Ground, Nottingham. However, with several other contenders vying for places in Birmingham's front-line, including Don Weston, Johnny Gordon, Jim Barrett and even Peter Murphy, surprisingly he made only 19 appearances at senior level that season, followed by 15 in 1960–61 when he claimed two goals in a 5–0 home win over Boldklub Copenhagen in the second round, second leg of the Fairs Cup at St Andrew's.

Still unable to hold down a regular place in the first team, Stubbs played in only eight games in 1961–62 and 15 in his last season of 1962–63 when Blues won the League Cup, beating Aston Villa 3–1 in the two-leg Final. He did not appear in any of the encounters against the old enemy, but he did help Blues get through earlier rounds against Barrow and Notts County.

In August 1963 Stubbs left St Andrew's – and the big question a lot of people asked at the time was why? For his record as a striker was very impressive – 20 goals scored in 71 first-class outings. Moving some 200 miles south to Torquay United for £6,000, he became a huge favourite with the Plainmoor fans, giving them plenty to cheer about, especially after setting a new club record with a five-timer in an 8–3 win over Newport County. He spent six years with the Gulls before having a spell with Bristol Rovers (July 1969 to February 1972). He then returned to Plainmoor in a swap deal involving future Port Vale manager John Rudge, and went on to take his overall goal tally to 133 in 263 competitive games for the Devon club before retiring in May 1974 after failing to recover from a cartilage operation.

Stubbs became a salesman in Torquay where he still resides, not too far away from Plainmoor, and continues to follow football, albeit via the newspapers or from the pleasure of his armchair in front of his television set.

Simon Sturridge

Date of birth: 9 December 1969, Birmingham

Blues record:
Appearances: League 129+21, FA Cup 8, League Cup 10+4, others 14
Goals: League 30, FA Cup 2, League Cup 1, others 5
Debut: League, 15 October 1988 v West Bromwich Albion (h) lost 4–1

Also played for: Stoke City, Blackpool, Northampton Town, Shrewsbury Town

Simon Sturridge's career in professional football spanned 12 years, during which time he scored 56 goals in a total of 314 first-class matches with four different clubs. Born and bred in Birmingham, and a pupil at William Cowper, Duddeston Manor and St George's Schools, he had scored plenty of goals in local Sunday League football before joining the apprentice ranks at St Andrew's in June 1985, turning professional in July 1988. Nurtured along gently, he made a big impression in Blues' youth and reserve teams before manager Garry Pendrey handed him his League debut as a second-half substitute in place of the injured Gary Childs in a 4–1 home defeat by Midland neighbours West Bromwich Albion in October 1988.

Sturridge made his first start in the front line the following month at home to Portsmouth and ended that season with 22 senior outings under his belt with three goals scored, the first against his future club Shrewsbury in March 1989 when Blues, heading rapidly towards the Third Division, lost 2–1.

Dave Mackay replaced Pendrey as manager in the summer, and he selected Sturridge in his side for the opening fixture in the Third Division at home to Crewe Alexandra. Blues won the contest 3–0 with Sturridge featuring on the score sheet, along with his co-striker Dennis Bailey and midfielder Mark Yates. Blues battled hard and long without really hitting top form and finished a disappointing seventh in the table, Sturridge netting 10 goals, as well as claiming another in the FA Cup tie against Leyton Orient.

After moderate performances by the team and most of the players during the first half of 1990–91, Mackay was replaced in the hot seat by Lou Macari, who quickly made changes to his line up, Sturridge retaining his place in the front line and going on to claim seven goals in total to finish up as the club's leading scorer in another disappointing League campaign as Blues languished in 12th place. There was some enjoyment, however, when Blues reached Wembley for the first time since 1956 when they met Tranmere Rovers in the Final of the Leyland DAF Cup, Sturridge scoring as his side went on to win 3–2 before a crowd of almost 59,000.

Another change of manager brought in the former Leeds United and England left-back Terry Cooper, who stuck with Sturridge in Birmingham's front line, initially partnering him with big John Gayle, but Gayle got injured and as a result Simon was, in effect, the senior striker, and he did a good job with a variety of others up front, including the adaptable Nigel Gleghorn, helping Blues finish runners-up in the table and so regain their Second Division status, Sturridge netting 10 goals in the process. Sharp and decisive with a good turn of foot, he was not at his best in 1992–93, struggling with injury and a loss of form as Blues battled to stay in the Second Division. He made only 20 League appearances (five as a substitute) and scored just one goal as Cooper bought in some new faces including Canadian international Paul Peschisolido and fiery Scotsman David Speedie.

In September 1993, after notching 38 goals in 186 games for Blues, Sturridge was transferred to Stoke City, where he remained for six years, joining Northampton Town in August 1999, after a loan spell at Blackpool. A year later he had a similar spell with Shrewsbury Town before quitting League football prior to the 2000–01 season.

Simon's younger brother Dean played for Derby County, Leicester City, Torquay United, Wolverhampton Wanderers and Sheffield United between 1991 and 2005, and his older brother Michael played for Blues and Wrexham.

Phil Summerrill

Date of birth: 20 November 1947, Erdington, Birmingham

Blues record:
Appearances: League 108+10, FA Cup 2+2, League Cup 8, others 0+1
Goals: League 46, FA Cup 2, League Cup 4, others 0
Debut: League, 18 March 1967 v Carlisle United (h) lost 2–1

Also played for: Huddersfield Town, Millwall, Wimbledon, Highgate United (two spells), Atherstone Town, Redditch United

Phil Summerrill was a true Brummie, a Blues man through and through, whose scoring record of 52 goals in 131 first-class matches has proved to be one of the best returns for the club since the late 1930s.

Summerrill was top marksman three seasons running, netting 17 goals in 1968–69 (the same number as Fred Pickering), following up with 13 in 1969–70 and notching 21 in 1970–71. He registered three hat-tricks during that time. The first came in a 5–2 home League win over Hull City in November 1968, the second in a 5–0 victory over Bolton Wanderers, also at St Andrew's, in March 1969, and the third away to Carlisle United in January 1970 when Blues lost 4–3.

A pupil at Kings Rise School, Summerrill represented Aston Boys and had the chance of joining Aston Villa before becoming an apprentice with Blues in June 1963, turning professional in December 1964. Steadily monitored through the youth and reserve teams at St Andrew's, he made his League debut on the left wing, wearing the number-11 shirt in a Second Division home game against Carlisle United in March 1967 – a month after Blues had lost their League Cup semi-final to Queen's Park Rangers. He appeared in the last two games of that season against Cardiff City and Charlton and had only one outing in 1967–68 against Norwich City before making his mark as a first-team regular in 1968–69 when he figured in a fluent forward line that also included Johnny Vincent, Trevor Hockey, Fred Pickering and Jimmy Greenhoff.

Summerrill was used predominantly on the left by manager Stan Cullis, but drifted inside to great effect, feeding off knockdowns from Pickering and Greenhoff. In fact, this strike-trio between them contributed 49 goals that season. In 1969–70 Tony Hateley, and at times Bob Latchford, partnered him up front but this time round the goals were hard to come by as Blues struggled to get their game together, finishing a disappointing 18th in the Second Division table.

It was all change, however, in 1970–71 as manager Freddie Goodwin, who had taken over from Cullis, installed Summerrill and Latchford as his main strike force, asking Trevor Francis to get forward as often as possible – and things improved greatly out on the pitch as Blues edged up to ninth in the table and scored 70 goals in League and Cup competitions.

Summerrill started the 1971–72 promotion-winning campaign as first-choice striker and played in eight of the opening 13 League games before losing his place in the team to Bob Hatton. He stuck in there, acting as first reserve, and had two outings the following season. Then, with his days numbered at St Andrew's, in January 1973 he moved north to join Huddersfield Town, switching to Millwall in November 1974 and on to the League's newcomers Wimbledon in September 1977. He remained with the Plough Lane Wombles until May 1979 when he returned to the Midlands to sign for Highgate United, later assisting Atherstone Town, Redditch United and Highgate again, eventually quitting football in 1986, although afterwards he did occasionally turn out in a handful of charity matches.

Summerrill, who still resides in Birmingham, went on to become a soccer coach, engaged at a youth centre in Sparkhill, which he did in his spare time when free from his painting and decorating business. Later in life he took employment in the local council's Football Coaching Department and is a regular visitor to St Andrew's.

Gordon Taylor

Date of birth: 28 December 1944, Ashton-under-Lyne, Lancashire

Blues record:
Appearances: League 156+10, FA Cup 16+1, League Cup 8+2, others 9+1
Goals: League 9, FA Cup 0, League 0, others 1
Debut: League, 19 December 1970 v Carlisle United (h) won 1–0

Also played for: Ashton Curzon, Bolton Wanderers, Blackburn Rovers, Vancouver Whitecaps (NASL), Bury

Gordon Taylor was a short, stocky, eager-beaver sort of player, fast and tricky, who loved to have the ball fed to his feet. He would then attempt to take his opposing full-back on a deep run, starting quite often from inside his own half of the field, and try to carry on before either checking back or crossing directly into the penalty area for one his strikers, and during his career he had plenty of quality centre-forwards to aim at. His appetite for work out on the pitch was second to none, and there is no doubt that he enjoyed his football.

Educated at Mossley Road County Primary and Ashton-under-Lyne Grammar Schools, Taylor, who started out as an inside-left, once scored 97 goals in a season as a 14-year-old and went on to captain Ashton Boys to the sixth round of the English Schools Trophy, also appearing three times for Lancashire Boys. Both Arsenal and Manchester United showed interest in him at the time, but after playing a season with Ashton Curzon he decided to join Bolton Wanderers as an amateur in June 1960, turning professional at Burnden Park in January 1962.

Taylor, who was switched to the left wing by Bolton, was an ever present in 1964–65 and went on to score 46 goals in 186 appearances for the Lancashire club before transferring to Blues for £18,000 in December 1970. He settled down quickly at St Andrew's and, after netting once, in a 2–0 home win over Bristol City, in 21 outings, he scored once more the following season in 30 League games to help Blues gain promotion to the First Division, and he played his part, too, in Blues surge to the FA Cup semi-finals, where they lost 1–0 to Leeds United at Hillsborough.

Taylor made 43 senior appearances in 1973–74 and added 47 to his tally the following season when yet again he and Blues missed out in the semi-finals of the FA Cup, losing this time to Fulham after a replay. A change of manager (Willie Bell taking over from Freddie Goodwin) resulted in a new formation being introduced, at which point Taylor was omitted from the side as Bell opted for a 4–3–3 system, using Trevor Francis, Peter Withe and Bob Hatton as his main strikers with Terry Hibbitt, Alan Campbell and Howard Kendall in midfield, later including Gary Emmanuel as well.

In March 1976 Taylor left St Andrew's, returning to Lancashire to sign for Blackburn Rovers, later assisting Vancouver Whitecaps in the NASL before switching to Bury – his fourth English club beginning with the letter B. He eventually retired from competitive football in May 1980 with 622 League and Cup appearances behind him to concentrate on working for the Professional Footballers Association, where he became secretary, later moving up the ladder to take over as chief executive, earning around £700,000 a year.

Taylor gained a Bachelor of Science degree in economics as a Bolton player (as insurance for his future, perhaps as a teacher), and he also passed his FA coaching badge, but never got round to using it, taking an internal job in football rather than staying outside!

Taylor's father and grandfather were avid Bolton supporters and both held season tickets at Burnden Park for many years, while Gordon himself supported the Wanderers from a very early age and was over the moon when he joined the club as a teenager.

Martin Thomas

Date of birth: 28 November 1959, Senghenydd near Caerphilly, South Wales

Blues record:

Appearances: League 144, FA Cup 7, League Cup 12, others 13
Goals: 0
Debut: League, 4 October 1988 v Plymouth Argyle (h) lost 1–0

Also played for: Bristol Rovers, Cardiff City (loan), Tottenham Hotspur (loan), Southend United (loan), Newcastle United, Middlesbrough (loan), Aston Villa (loan), Crystal Palace (loan), Cheltenham Town and Wales (5 Youth, 2 Under-21 and 1 full cap)

A Blues legend? Yes, certainly – despite playing in a struggling side and suffering with niggling injuries. Welshman Martin Thomas made 176 first-team appearances in six years with the club, and although erratic at times he was nonetheless a very competent goalkeeper, comfortable on his line, superb with reactive saves and efficient with high crosses, choosing to punch the ball to safety perhaps far too often, rather than catching it.

A product of the 'Welsh' nursery at Bristol Rovers, for whom he initially signed as an apprentice in June 1975, turning professional in September 1976, Thomas was voted Player of the Year by the Rovers supporters in his first full season at Eastville, and he became a firm favourite after that, going on to amass 183 first-team appearances as well as collecting two Under-21 caps for Wales, lining up against England in 1979 and Holland in 1981.

Thomas lost his place in the Rovers team due to a dislocated finger, which kept him out of action for almost a year. When he regained full fitness, he found Phil Kite barring his way between the posts, and after a loan spells with Cardiff City (July–November 1982), Tottenham Hotspur (December 1982), Southend United (February 1983) and Newcastle United (March 1983) he joined the latter club on a permanent basis for £50,000 four months later. He went on to appear in 131 senior games for the Geordies, gained his only senior cap for his country versus Finland in 1987 when regular 'keeper Neville Southall and two reserves, Andy Dibble and Tony Norman, were all unavailable for various reasons. He also helped Newcastle clinch promotion from the Second Division in his first full season at St James' Park, but after that he had to jockey for his position with Kevin Carr and, in fact, was loaned out to Middlesbrough (October–November 1984) to keep fit before becoming number one.

In October 1988, having been in the second city earlier in the year when on loan to Aston Villa, Thomas was recruited, initially on loan, by Blues manager Garry Pendrey to replace Tony Godden, and shortly afterwards became a permanent signing at £75,000. But despite some dodgy performances as well as some excellent ones – he kept 14 clean sheets – Blues unfortunately were relegated to the Third Division. In March of that season, during the home game with Shrewsbury Town, he conceded a bizarre own-goal whereby, after gathering a high ball, he stepped back over his own line, ball still in his hands, and presented the Shrews an undeserved 2–1 victory.

A change of manager saw Dave Mackay take over the reins, and he kept Thomas as his first choice 'keeper, as did his successor (from January 1991) Lou Macari. He missed only four League games in 1989–90 and one the following season when his penalty saves against Swansea City were a major factor in Blues going on to win the Leyland DAF Cup at Wembley when he produced an outstanding performance as Tranmere Rovers were defeated 3–2. However, a third of the way through the 1991–92 campaign, after a few injury worries, he came under pressure, and with another new manager on board in Terry Cooper he was subsequently replaced by Kevin Miller.

Thomas was loaned out to Crystal Palace during the 1992–93 season, and having failed to regain his place in Blues' first team he left St Andrew's for Cheltenham Town in August 1994. After retiring 12 months later with over 400 senior appearances to his credit, he became a specialised goalkeeping coach, assisting Blues, Swindon Town and Newcastle United while also being engaged by the FA at their Lilleshall training HQ.

Thomas's brother David played for Wales B at rugby union.

Colin Todd

Date of birth: 12 December 1948, Chester-le-Street, County Durham

Blues record:
Appearances: League 92+1, FA Cup 7, League Cup 8
Goals: 0
Debut: League, 22 September 1979, as a substitute v Leyton Orient (a) drew 2–2

Also played for: Sunderland, Derby County, Everton, Nottingham Forest, Oxford United, Vancouver Whitecaps (NASL), Luton Town and England (3 Youth, 14 Under-23 and 27 full caps)
Managed: Whitley Bay, Middlesbrough, Bolton Wanderers, Swindon Town, Derby County and Bradford City

Colin Todd began his professional career with Sunderland, for whom he made his League debut at the age of 17 while still an apprentice. An FA Youth Cup winner in 1967, he missed only one senior game in 1968–69 when he also gained the first of 14 England Under-23 caps when only 19 years old. He was absent from first-team duty very rarely over the next few years, and after amassing 191 senior appearances for the Wearsiders he joined Derby County for £180,000 in February 1971. He twice helped the Rams win the Football League title, first in 1972 and then in 1975. He also collected a winners' medal when the Texaco Cup was lifted in 1972, the same year he won his first full England cap versus Northern Ireland. His 27th and last was to follow five years later against the same country.

In 1975 Todd had the honour of being voted PFA Footballer of the Year. After making 371 League and Cup appearances for the Rams (10 goals scored) he moved 50 miles north to Everton in September 1978 for £333,000.

Elegant, self-assured, confident, able to defend or work in midfield, Todd was a superb reader of the game, was never flustered, could pass and head the ball as good as anyone in the game, and, above all, he was a true professional, very rarely getting in trouble with the referee.

Todd never settled down on Merseyside and made only 35 first-class appearances for Everton before transferring to Blues for £300,000 in September, signed by Jim Smith to replace Terry Lees in what, at the time, was proving to be the difficult right-back berth. He spent three excellent seasons at St Andrew's, starring, yes starring – a word that can be used without hesitation – in 108 competitive games, mainly as a central-defender. He helped Blues regain their place in the First Division in 1980 when he formed a terrific partnership at the back with Joe Gallagher. The following season he again did superbly well as Blues consolidated themselves in the top flight. Then, expected or not, he was lured away by his former manager Brian Clough to Nottingham Forest for just £70,000.

Todd spent 18 months at the City Ground before switching south to Oxford United, going on later to assist Vancouver Whitecaps (May–October 1984) and finally Luton Town, announcing his retirement in May 1985 with over 800 senior appearances under his belt, 641 in the Football League. He actually made his 500th League appearance as a Blues player against Swansea City in October 1979, and five years later he became the oldest player ever to appear in a senior game for Oxford United, aged 35.

After starting his managerial career in non-League football with Whitley Bay, Todd became youth-team coach at Middlesbrough in May 1986, and following a spell as assistant manager to Bruce Rioch he was handed full control of team affairs at Ayresome Park in March 1990, holding his position until the following June. In January 1992 he was appointed assistant boss at Bradford City, switching to Bolton Wanderers in the same capacity in May 1992, moving up to joint manager with his former Derby County playing colleague Roy McFarland in January 1995 before making the position his own in November 1996.

After taking Bolton up and then bringing them down from the Premiership in 1997 and 1998 respectively, Todd left the Reebok Stadium the following year and was out of the game for a short while before returning in April 2000 as manager of relegated Swindon Town, briefly moving into the hot seat at Derby in August 2001 to January 2002, before taking charge of Bradford City in June 2004.

Dan Tremelling

Date of birth: 12 November 1899, Mansfield Woodhouse, Nottinghamshire
Died: 15 August 1970, Birmingham

Blues record:
Appearances: League 382, FA Cup 13, Wartime 2
Goals: 0
Debut: Wartime Subsidiary Competition, 19 April v Leicester Fosse (h) won 3–0
Senior debut: League, 30 August 1919 v Hull City (h) won 4–1

Also played for: Langwith Junction Wagon Works, Shirebrook Juniors, Lincoln City, Bury and England (1 full cap)

Dan Tremelling was a fixture in the Blues goal for a decade, being wonderfully consistent – he actually made more League and FA Cup appearances for the club than Harry Hibbs (395 to 388). He was brilliant at catching high balls, was a safe-handler of ground shots, and he was also courageous and gave great assurance to the defenders in front of him. A former miner near his home town of Mansfield, he played for the Langwith Junction Wagon Works team and had brief spells with Shirebrook Juniors and Lincoln City (August 1918) before joining Blues in April 1919 as a guest, signing permanently two months later. He played in two regional games at the end of that 1918–19 season (both against Leicester Fosse) before making his senior debut on the opening Saturday of the first peacetime League campaign after World War One, having taken over from Bruce Godfrey.

In Tremelling's first full season at St Andrew's, Blues finished third in Division Two. He missed quite a few games through injury in 1920–21 but in the end his 30 League outings earned him a Second Division Championship medal, and the following season he was absent just three times, helping Blues hold on to their top-flight status.

Between August 1919 and April 1929, Blues fulfilled 420 League games and Dan played in 370 of them. He was outstanding between the posts, receiving high praise from visiting managers and players alike. He was an ever present on three occasions, 1919–20, 1923–24 and 1924–25, and missed only one game in 1925–26 and two in 1922–23. Something of an expert at saving penalties, his last minute spot-kick save from Len Davies of Cardiff City in the final game of the 1923–24 season at St Andrew's prevented the Welsh club from winning the League title. The game ended level at 0–0, whereas a victory would have taken Cardiff a point ahead of the subsequent champions Huddersfield Town.

With Jack Brown (Sheffield Wednesday) and Ted Hufton (West Ham) out of action, Tremelling won his only full cap for England in November 1927 in a 2–1 defeat by Wales at Burnley. After that he was named as a reserve on three occasions but did manage to play three times for the Football League against the Irish League in 1927 (1) and 1928 (2).

Forever bouncing up and down on his line, Tremelling was affectionately known as the India Rubber Man, and if he did produce a bad performance it is said that he was, at times, inconsolable and would go into hiding for a few days. Having lost his place in the first team to Harry Hibbs, he remained at St Andrew's until May 1932 when he joined Bury. Retiring at the end of the 1935–36 season, he was invited back by Blues as assistant-trainer, a position he retained until September 1941. He later ran the Old Lodge pub near St Andrew's.

One interesting point from a statistical angle is that the number-13 was certainly not unlucky for Tremelling. He joined Blues on the 13th of the month and left on the 13th; his 13th League game was against Wolves (won 2–0); he spent exactly 13 years at St Andrew's and played in 13 FA Cup ties.

Tremelling's brother William played as a defender and forward for Blackpool (1924–30) and Preston North End (1930–37). He made a total of 323 League appearances and scored 54 goals, gaining an FA Cup runners'-up medal in 1937 against Sunderland.

Cyril Trigg

Date of birth:	8 April 1917, Measham, Leicestershire
Died:	9 April 1993, Birmingham

Blues record:

Appearances:	League 268, FA Cup 23, Wartime 95
Goals:	League 67, FA Cup 5, Wartime 87
Debut:	League, 28 March 1936 v Aston Villa (a) lost 2–1

Also played for: Binley Welfare, Coventry City (trial), Blackpool (guest), Nottingham Forest (guest), Stourbridge (player-coach)

Cyril Trigg played through three generations of Blues teams, witnessing relegation, promotion, success and failure all down the line. He saw many changes at the club, played under four different managers, occupied a variety of positions from full-back to centre-forward, yet still came up smiling. A great competitor, as a defender he was rugged, resilient, dogged and determined, while as a forward he was a pest, causing all sorts of problems in the opposing penalty area with his aggressive style and powerful shooting. He was also strong in the air and once headed a goal from 20 yards.

A dedicated club man, 'Triggy', as he was called by virtually everyone at St Andrew's, was at one stage simultaneously the best full-back and centre-forward at the club, and during World War Two, when he played as a guest for Blackpool and Nottingham Forest when on leave from his duties with the RAF in India and Burma, he appeared in almost 100 first-team matches for the club, scoring 87 goals. One wonders what he might have achieved had Hitler and his troops not invaded Europe.

Born during World War One, Trigg was an amateur trialist with Coventry City before joining Bedworth Town in 1934, from where he moved to Blues, initially as a junior, in August 1935, turning professional three months later. He made his League debut at right-back (in place of Ned Barkas) in the second city derby against rivals Aston Villa (away) in March 1936 when a crowd of 50,000 saw Blues beaten 2–1. He was handed three more outings that season before making the position his own in 1936–37 when he was partnered by first Billy Steel then by Barkas and late on by Billy Hughes. In fact, on 27 March 1937 they created a new record for being the youngest-ever pair of full-backs to appear together in the same Football League game when they faced Preston North End at St Andrew's, a game Blues won 1–0.

Trigg made 111 League and FA Cup appearances for Blues before the hostilities, suffering relegation in 1939, the same year he lined up against Everton when a record crowd of 67,341 packed into St Andrew's to see the 2–2 fifth-round FA Cup draw with Everton. And after the fighting had ended, he went on to add a further 180 to his tally, netting, in total, 72 goals, his first – the winner – coming against Middlesbrough in a home League game on Boxing Day 1938 (2–1). He gained a Football League South Championship-winners' medal in 1946 (when Blues pipped rivals Villa on a goal average for the title), played in that season's FA Cup semi-final (beaten by Derby County after a replay) and two years later helped Blues win the Second Division title, when he made 25 appearances, seven at right-back and 18 as centre-forward, from where he struck six goals, two of them proving to be vital under the circumstances. He made a second appearance in an FA Cup semi-final in 1951 but once again it ended in disappointment for all concerned as Blues went out to Blackpool after another replay. That season saw him equal his best scoring record for Blues (19 goals), having claimed the same total in 1946–47. The following campaign he was virtually regarded as a reserve (to new signing Tommy Briggs) before bouncing back in 1952–53 with 11 senior goals, adding five more to his tally in season 1953–54, at the end of which he left the club to become player-coach at Stourbridge, retiring from football in May 1957. He still maintained his fitness and was a regular visitor to St Andrew's for many years until poor health caught up with him in 1988. Cyril was 76 when he died.

Johnny Vincent

Date of birth: 8 February 1947, West Bromwich

Blues record:
Appearances: League 168+3, FA Cup 11+1, League Cup 11
Goals: League 41, FA Cup 0, League Cup 3
Debut: League, 13 March 1964 v Blackburn Rovers (h) drew 2–2

Also played for: Middlesbrough, Cardiff City, Atherstone Town, Connecticut Bi-Centennials (NASL) and England (5 Youth caps)

Johnny Vincent supported West Bromwich Albion as a youngster – so too did his family and a lot of his Black Country friends. He represented Brierley Hill Schoolboys before joining Blues as an apprentice in June 1962, turning professional on his 17th birthday in February 1964 – a month before he was handed his League debut, taking over at inside-right in the absence of Jimmy Bloomfield against Blackburn Rovers in March 1964 – this being the first of 194 senior appearances for Blues (44 goals scored in total).

Nurtured along in the intermediate and reserve teams at St Andrew's, Vincent gained five England Youth caps and eventually established himself as a regular member of Blues' first XI during the second half of the 1966–67 season, under manager Stan Cullis who, in his time as boss of Wolves, had been involved with some truly great scheming midfielders, players like Peter Broadbent and to a certain extent Ron Flowers, both of whom could also attack a bit. He linked up in the engine room with Trevor Hockey and Ron Wylie, both of whom had Aston Villa connections during their careers. He also had a wide man, a winger, to feed into Bert Murray as well some useful strikers in Barry Bridges and Geoff Vowden, another Villa man.

Vincent did splendidly this term, helping Blues reach the semi-final stage of the League Cup with an impressive quarter-final performance against Sheffield United when he scored a fine goal in a 3–2 win. Unfortunately he was disappointed not to play against Third Division Queen's Park Rangers in the two-leg semi-final, a fixture the Londoners won convincingly 7–2 on aggregate.

The following season (1967–68) Vincent missed only a handful of League matches, netting 14 goals, including one in each of the opening three games, as Blues once again reached a major Cup semi-final. This time, after some very impressive displays against quality opposition, they met his boyhood heroes West Bromwich Albion at neutral Villa Park in the last four of the FA Cup competition. Despite his promptings and his general midfield aggression when challenged by Doug Fraser, Ian Collard and company, Blues went down 2–0 against the eventual winners of the trophy. During this period he had the former Everton striker Fred Pickering to aim his passes at up front, while Bridges was the main off-the-ball runner, collecting Vincent's long passes hit down the channels, a job he did exceedingly well.

A natural ball player, fairly tall for a footballer in his position, Vincent had excellent vision. He was a smart passer, short or long, who could deliver a telling cross as well as being able to fire in a ferocious shot, predominantly with his right foot, which he used to great effect when the opportunity presented itself. He certainly orchestrated things in centre-field, and he did so with some quality, pitting his wits and pulling the strings against some of the best players in the land. He missed only one League game in 1968–69 and six the following season, but then, after 22 outings in 1970–71, Blues manager Freddie Goodwin surprised a lot of people by selling him to Middlesbrough for a fee of £40,000 in March 1971, bringing in a much harder man in George Smith.

Johnny later switched to South Wales, joining Cardiff City in October 1972 for £55,000, collecting a Welsh Cup-winners' medal at the end of that season. After spells with Atherstone Town (from August 1975) and Connecticut Bi-Centennials in the NASL during season 1977–78, he decided to hang up his boots at the age of 31, basically through injury – he had suffered with a tedious knee problem for a little over a year.

Later in life Vincent, who remained in the Midlands, became a licensee, acting as mine host of the Travellers' Rest in Northfield, Birmingham, and also ran pubs deep in his home territory (the Black Country) in Oldbury and Warley.

Geoff Vowden

Date of birth: 27 April 1941, Barnsley, Yorkshire

Blues record:
Appearances: League 213+8, FA Cup 16, League Cup 16
Goals: League 79, FA Cup 8, League Cup 7
Debut: League, 24 October 1964 v Blackpool (h) won 3–0

Also played for: Jersey DM FC, Nottingham Forest, Aston Villa, Kettering Town (player-assistant manager) and New York Cosmos (NASL)

Various match-day programmes during the 1960s described Geoff Vowden as follows: 'A tremendous striker, who could score goals with both feet and also his head,' 'A beautifully balanced player who can also occupy a midfield position if required' and 'A fine marksman who enjoys playing alongside a big centre-forward.' He was certainly a versatile performer whose professional career spanned some 14 years, during which time he netted well over 150 goals in a shade under 500 senior matches, including 94 strikes in 253 competitive games for Blues. He is currently lying in seventh place in the list of the club's all-time goalscorers.

A Yorkshireman, born close to a colliery in Barnsley, Vowden was brought up on the Channel Island of Jersey, where he played a lot of intermediate football before joining Nottingham Forest as an amateur in the summer of 1958, turning professional in January 1960 under manager Billy Walker, who was a star forward with Aston Villa during the 1920s.

Vowden netted 48 goals in 108 senior games for Forest before transferring to Blues for a fee of £25,000 in October 1964. Four years later he got his name in the record books by becoming the first substitute to come off the bench and score a hat-trick in League football. He replaced the injured Ron Wyle during the Second Division game against Huddersfield Town at St Andrew's on 7 September 1968, helping Blues to an emphatic 5–1 win. In between times he had done very well in a struggling Blues side. Despite netting on his senior debut against Blackpool and finishing up as joint top scorer with 10 goals in 27 League games, his first season at St Andrew's ended with Blues being relegated from the top flight. Undeterred, like his teammates, he followed up his efforts in 1965–66 by becoming leading marksman with 23 goals in 40 senior outings, going on to claim another 21 in 48 competitive games in 1966–67 when Blues were defeated 7–2 by Queen's Park Rangers in the two-leg League Cup semi-final.

In season 1967–68, and by now at the peak of his form, feeding off burly centre-forward Fred Pickering (ex-Everton and England) and taking in his stride the pin-point passes delivered to him by midfielder Johnny Vincent and the crosses provided from both flanks, Vowden weighed in with another 21 goals (in 48 starts), helping Blues reach the semi-final of the FA Cup, scoring in rounds three, four and five against Halifax Town, Leyton Orient and Arsenal respectively. Unfortunately his hopes of appearing at Wembley were dashed as neighbours West Bromwich Albion won the semi-final showdown at Villa Park 2–0.

Vowden continued to find the net but was not quite so prolific, claiming just seven goals in 27 games in 1968–69 (including that treble as a sub) and grabbing six more in 33 matches the following season, by which time he was being used mainly behind the two chosen strikers Phil Summerill and Tony Hateley, although late on he got back into the side in place of the injured Hateley.

Freddie Goodwin took over as Blues manager in the summer of 1970, and he immediately started to alter things around on the pitch, and after scoring six goals in 23 appearances during the first half of that campaign Vowden found himself surplus to requirements, eventually moving to rivals Aston Villa in March 1971 for £12,500. He spent three years at Villa Park, gaining a Third Division Championship-winners' medal in 1972 before entering non-League football with Kettering Town in July 1974 as player and assistant manager. He rounded off his playing career in the States with New York Cosmos and later took on a coaching position in Saudi Arabia as well as running soccer classes for schoolboys in and around Nottingham. In 1980–81 he acted as reserve-team coach at Sheffield United.

Roy Warhurst

Date of birth: Handsworth, Sheffield, 18 September 1926

Blues record:

Appearances: League 213, FA Cup 23, European 3
Goals: League 10, FA Cup 0, European 0
Debut: League, 18 March 1950 v Manchester City (h) drew 0–0

Also played for: Atlas & Norfolk FC (Sheffield), Huddersfield Town (amateur), Sheffield United, Manchester City, Oldham Athletic, Banbury Spencer

Roy Warhurst started his career as an out-and-out winger, neat and tidy with some good skills, before developing into a stocky, wavy-haired wing-half with a bone-crunching tackle, a destroyer of the highest degree, the sort of player any manager would love to have in his side. He never pulled out of a 50–50 challenge, no matter who his opponent was. He was totally committed, produced nothing less than 100 percent each and every time he took the field, and, above all, he was a down-to-earth character, a big hit with the fans and his teammates alike and a footballer who simply loved and enjoyed the game.

A Yorkshireman, born in the district of Handsworth on the outskirts of Sheffield, Warhurst was an amateur with Huddersfield Town before going on to make 17 first-class appearances in almost six years as a professional with Sheffield United, who signed him initially in May 1944, upgrading him five months later. When he chose to switch his allegiance to St Andrew's in March 1950, for what proved to be a bargain price of just £8,000, he was regarded, and indeed listed, as an orthodox outside-left, recruited as cover for Harry Roberts. Indeed, during the first three-quarters of that relegation season, struggling Blues had already named nine different players in the troublesome left-wing position. Roy was the 10th, and he had three outings wearing the number-11 shirt over a period of four weeks, the first in front of 30,000 fans at St Andrew's when Manchester City scrounged a point from a 1–1 draw.

Playing in the reserves for most of 1950–51, Warhurst finally claimed a regular place in the first XI at left-half in September 1951, taking over from Ray Ferris. He never looked back, and, with fellow half-backs Len Boyd and Trevor Smith alongside him, he and Blues began to produce the goods. He made 38 League and Cup appearances in 1951–52 and scored the first of his 10 goals for the club in a 4–2 win at Luton in early December. The following season he had 37 outings, missing 11 League games through injury, before adding 38 more to his total in 1953–54. He was then instrumental in helping Blues win the Second Division Championship in 1954–55, missing only eight League games (mainly through injury), and he also managed to score four goals, three in the first four matches, including a point-saver away to Bristol Rovers.

The following season Blues reached the FA Cup Final at Wembley, but sadly, after starring in each of the first four rounds, Warhurst missed the semi-final win over Sunderland and then had the disappointment of missing out on the Final too, his place going to Johnny Newman. Some say his absence was a crucial factor as Blues lost 3–1 to Manchester City. After scoring 10 goals in 239 senior appearances for Blues, it was a surprise to a lot of people, certainly the fans at St Andrew's (and even those at Maine Road), when iron-man Roy was transferred to Manchester City in the summer of 1957. He spent almost two years with City, making 41 first-team appearances before serving Crewe Alexandra from March 1959 to August 1960, playing in 55 games. He rounded off his first-class career with Oldham Athletic in 1960–61, making a further eight appearances. He then had a useful spell in non-League football with Banbury Spencer before retiring in May 1964 at the age of 38. He amassed 360 League and Cup appearances during his playing days, and it was not for the want of trying that he failed to win a representative honour. He worked as a scrap metal dealer in Lichfield for many years after his footballing days were over.

Johnny Watts

Date of birth:	13 April 1931, Vauxhall, Birmingham
Died:	12 March 2006, Birmingham

Blues record:

Appearances:	League 206, FA Cup 17, League Cup 8, Europe 17
Goals:	League 3, FA Cup 0, League Cup 0, Europe 0
Debut:	League, 16 February 1952 v Swansea Town (a) lost 4–0

Also played for: Saltley Old Boys, Nuneaton Borough and Bromsgrove Rovers

Wing-half Johnny Watts joined Blues as an amateur in August 1948, turned professional three years later in August 1951 and made his League debut in a Second Division game at Swansea two months before his 21st birthday when he deputised for Len Boyd in a 4–0 defeat. This was not the greatest of starts for him as a League footballer, but he quickly got over that shock introduction and went on to serve Blues superbly well for another 11 years, eventually leaving St Andrew's in July 1963 – just after the League Cup had been won at Aston Villa's expense – although he didn't feature in the Final.

Strong and competitive, energetic and courageous, Watts, who could also occupy the centre-half position, performed the sliding tackle to perfection, rarely committing a foul – although he did, on two occasions in the mid-1950s, concede penalties in vital matches which cost Blues dearly, one for hand-ball, the other for a foul by pushing. His infamous sliding tackles, however, also brought him into conflict with several referees on the European circuit, who seemed to clamp down on such tactics when Blues were competing in the Inter Cities Fairs Cup competition between 1958 and 1961.

Initially spotted by Blues chief scout Walter Taylor playing local Sunday football on the Glebe Farm recreational ground near to his home in Birmingham, Watts gained a regular place in the first team at St Andrew's in 1956–57 after completing his national service. Effectively he took over the right-half berth from Len Boyd, although there were two others players – Johnny Newman and Bert Linnecor – challenging him for that spot.

Prior to that campaign, Watts had managed only 32 senior outings for Blues in five seasons, appearing in 10 League games when the Second Division Championship was won in 1954–55 and 10 more the following season when he sat in the stands at Wembley watching his teammates lose 3–1 to Manchester City in the 1956 FA Cup Final. In 1956–57 Blues came close to competing in a Wembley Final again, but this time, with Watts now bedded in the side at right-half, they lost to Manchester United's Busby Babes 2–0 in the semi-final at Hillsborough.

Owing to niggling injury problems, in 1957–58 Watts played in only half of Blues' senior games, but he did manage to score his first goal for the club, a classic drive in a 5–1 home League win over Bolton Wanderers. He was back to his best the following season when he was part of a very efficient half-back line that also included Trevor Smith and Dick Neal, making 48 appearances and netting his second goal in a thrilling 7–1 League victory over the subsequent FA Cup winners Nottingham Forest at the City Ground. He then added 46 outings to his tally in 1959–60 when he helped Blues reach the Fairs Cup Final, when they were beaten 4–1 on aggregate over two legs by the Spanish giants Barcelona. He made another 40 appearances in 1960–61, playing in the opening rounds of the Fairs Cup, only to miss out on a second Final appearance against AS Roma (lost 4–2 on aggregate). However, with Welsh international Terry Hennessey now preferred at right-half (wearing the number-four shirt), his last two seasons with Blues revealed just 23 first-class appearances, bringing his final tally to 248. He wound down his career with decent spells in non-League football with two Midlands clubs, Nuneaton Borough and Bromsgrove Rovers, before announcing his retirement in the summer of 1969 at the age of 38.

Watts remained in close contact with the club after that and often attended reunions for former players.

Jeff Wealands

Date of birth: 26 August 1951, Darlington

Blues record:
Appearances: League 102, FA Cup 5, League Cup 10, others 1+1
Goals: 0
Debut: League, 22 August 1979 v Sunderland (a) lost 2–0

Also played for: Cleveland Bridge FC, Wolverhampton Wanderers, Northampton Town (loan), Darlington, Hull City, Manchester United (loan), Oldham Athletic (loan), Preston North End (loan), Altrincham (two spells) and Barrow

Released by Wolverhampton Wanderers without making a first-team appearance at Molineux, goalkeeper Jeff Wealands also had a brief loan spell with Northampton Town before making his League debut for Darlington in August 1971. He moved from Feethams to Hull City for £10,000 on transfer deadline day in March 1972, and in his first season with the Tigers he shared the number-one position with long-time incumbent Ian MacKechnie before becoming the undisputed 'fixture' at Boothferry Park for four campaigns and an ever present in two of them.

Wealands, who went on to appear in 306 first-team games for Hull, was transferred to Blues in July 1979, signed for £30,000 by manager Jim Smith who, at the time, was slowly but surely assembling a promotion-winning side.

A capable, unspectacular 'keeper, Wealands took over from Neil Freeman and made 40 League appearances in his first season at St Andrew's, helping Blues regain their place in the top flight, finishing in third spot on goal average from Chelsea and only two points behind the champions Leicester City and one adrift of second-place Sunderland. He was also voted the club's Player of the Year – being one of only a few goalkeepers to receive this accolade. He remained in control and kept his form throughout 1980–81 (46 senior outings) and added 25 more games to his tally in 1981–82 when he was pushed all the way by the up and coming Tony Coton. Then Scotsman Jim Blyth arrived from Coventry City and at that point Wealands's career with Blues was put in jeopardy. Ron Saunders had taken over as manager, and in truth he preferred Coton as his number-one 'keeper, also hinting that he was looking for someone else! Rather disappointed, Wealands fell into dispute with the club and was loaned out to Manchester United in February 1983, where he deputised for the injured Gary Bailey, and he kept a clean sheet in his first two games. Signed permanently in August 1983 by manager Ron Atkinson, who had admired his displays for quite some time, he was troubled by a recurring back injury at Old Trafford, and after spending loan spells with Oldham Athletic (March–April 1984) and Preston North End (December 1984) he moved into a lower grade of football by signing for Altrincham in May 1985. He did extremely well at this level and helped the non-League club complete an FA Cup giant-killing act when they visited his old hunting ground at St Andrew's in January 1986 and knocked Blues out of the competition in the third round by 2–1. At the end of this very same season he gained a winners'-medal when he starred between the posts as Altrincham lifted the FA Trophy, beating Enfield 1–0 in a tightly-contested Final at Wembley.

Despite his ups and downs during the latter part of his career, Wealands proved to be a durable goalkeeper who remained in the game as a player until well past his 41st birthday. His most embarrassing moment as a goalkeeper came on 18 September 1973 when his counterpart Ray Cashley of Bristol City thumped the ball downfield and watched it sail over Wealands's head into the net to help his side register a 3–1 League victory over Hull City.

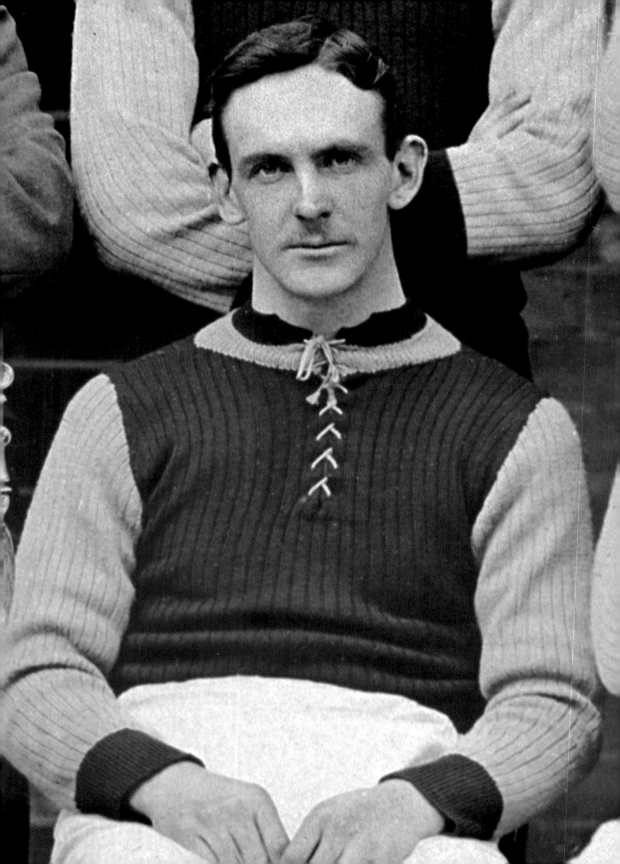

Fred Wheldon

Date of birth: 1 November 1869, Langley Green, Oldbury, Worcestershire
Died: 13 January 1924, St George's, Worcester

Blues record:
Appearances: League 79, Football Alliance 46, FA Cup 12, Test Matches 3
Goals: League 58, Football Alliance 34, FA Cup 12, Test Matches 2
Debut: Football Alliance, 15 February 1890 v Darwen (h) won 6–2; FA Cup, 4 October 1890 v Hednesford Town (h) won 8–0; Football League, 3 September 1892 v Burslem Port Vale (h) won 5–1

Also played for: Rood End White Star, Langley Green Victoria, Aston Villa, West Bromwich Albion (two spells, first on trial), Queen's Park Rangers, Portsmouth, Worcester City and England (4 full and 2 XI caps)

The youngest of 10 children, Fred 'Diamond' Wheldon was a brilliant footballer, an exceptional talent and a tremendous goalscorer, whose career spanned 16 years. He was the first ever player to appear in a League game for three major Midlands clubs, Blues, Aston Villa and West Bromwich Albion.

Regularly wearing a pair of golfing stockings instead of the football type, Wheldon played local football and had an unsuccessful trial with the then FA Cup holders West Bromwich Albion in 1888. Two years later, in mid-February 1890, he signed as a semi-professional for Blues, scoring twice on his senior debut within 48 hours in a 6–2 home win over Darwen in a Football Alliance fixture. In May 1890 he became a full-time professional and was an ever present in the side that campaign, scoring 14 goals, including his first hat-trick for the club in his first FA Cup tie, an 8–0 qualifying round win over Hednesford.

Forming a fine partnership on the left wing with first Billy Pratt and then Tommy Hands, Wheldon top scored the following season with 21 Alliance and eight FA Cup goals, helping Blues finish third in the table and so gain a place in the Football League. He played in Blues' first ever game in Division Two, grabbing two goals in a 5–1 home victory over Burslem Port Vale, thus having the pleasure of scoring on his debut in each of the three different major competitions. He was brilliant that season, rattling in 26 goals in total as Blues won the title, but he missed out on promotion after losing 6–3 on aggregate to Newton Heath (Manchester United) in the Test Matches (today's equivalent is the Play-offs). In 1893–94 he was superb again, notching 24 goals (22 in the League), gaining a second Division Two-winners' medal and this time promotion as Blues beat Darwen 3–1 in the Test Match at Stoke, Wheldon scoring one of the goals. Eleven more goals followed in 1894–95, including the club's first penalty in a 2–2 draw with Aston Villa, as Blues held their own in the top flight. He struck 10 more in 1895–96 to take him past the century mark in goals scored.

In June 1896 after six excellent years with Blues, Wheldon moved to a bigger stage, joining Aston Villa for £350. He maintained his form and scored 74 goals in 140 games over the next four seasons, helping Villa win three League titles (1897, 1898 and 1900) and the FA Cup, also in 1897 when, of course, the double was achieved. He won four England caps (1897 and 1898), played for an England XI twice and represented the Football League on four occasions versus the Irish League and Scottish League.

Wheldon joined West Bromwich Albion in August 1900 for £100 and appeared in the first League game at The Hawthorns against Derby County but was in a struggling team as the Baggies suffered relegation. In December 1901 Fred signed for Queen's Park Rangers and later served with Portsmouth from August 1902 to July 1904, before ending his career in May 1906 after two seasons with Worcester.

Besides his footballing exploits, Wheldon was also a fine cricketer who, between 1899 and 1906, scored 4,938 runs for Worcestershire at an average of 22.50. He struck three centuries and claimed 95 catches, some as a wicket-keeper. He also played for Carmarthen CC. He remained in Worcester for the rest of his life, working as a publican prior to his death in January 1924 at the age of 54. His brother Sam played for Albion, while his son Norris assisted Liverpool.

Colin Withers

Date of birth: 21 March 1940, Erdington, Birmingham

Blues record:
Appearances: League 98, FA Cup 7, League Cup 8, Europe 3
Goals: 0
Debut: League, 19 November 1960 v Tottenham Hotspur (a) lost 6–0

Also played for: Paget Rangers, West Bromwich Albion, Aston Villa, Lincoln City, Go Ahead Deventer (Holland), Atherstone Town and England (1 Schoolboy cap)

Birmingham-born goalkeeper Colin 'Tiny' Withers, who stood 6ft 3ins tall and weighed around 13st, was on the receiving end of a 6–0 drubbing when making his League debut for Blues against the subsequent double winners Tottenham Hotspur at White Hart Lane in 1960. Four days later he let in four more in a 4–4 draw with Boldklub Copenhagen in an Inter Cities Fairs Cup tie in Denmark. After that nightmare start, however, he became an exceptionally sound last line of defence. He helped Blues stave off relegation that season – they finished in 19th position and also reached the Fairs Cup Final when they were defeated over two legs by AS Roma, Withers acting as reserve in both games against the Italian club.

Withers contested the goalkeeping position with Johnny Schofield until taking over as first choice during the 1962–63 season when Blues won their first-ever major trophy, lifting the League Cup at the expense of his future club Aston Villa in the two-leg Final (won 3–1 on aggregate). Having appeared in the opening five games, including wins of 5–0 and 6–0 over Doncaster Rovers and Manchester City, he unfortunately missed the Final itself, former 'keeper and manager Gil Merrick electing to go with the more experienced Schofield. A brave and daring 'keeper, with a safe pair of hands, he made 31 senior appearances that season and missed only four League games in 1963–64, when once again he was involved in a dog-fight at the foot of the First Division table, Blues just managing to pull clear of relegation after winning their last two games against Liverpool and Sheffield United, both at home.

Capped by England at Schoolboy level versus Northern Ireland in 1954, Withers was initially a junior with Paget Rangers and also an amateur with West Bromwich Albion before being released by Baggies manager Vic Buckingham after three months – owing to the number of useful 'keepers at The Hawthorns at that time. Obviously disappointed, he jumped at the chance to join Blues as a full-time professional at the age of 17 in May 1957, signed by Arthur Turner. Nursed along by future England 'keeper Gil Merrick, he played well at both intermediate and reserve-team levels before establishing himself in the first XI. Remaining at St Andrew's for seven years, he was subsequently transferred to second city rivals Aston Villa for a fee of £18,000 in November 1964, having made 116 senior appearances for Blues.

Withers actually lost his place in the Blues team to his predecessor Schofield after just five games at the start of the 1964–65 League campaign and his first senior outing for his new club Villa was also in a Division One fixture against the same opponents he had come up against when starting out with Blues four years earlier – Tottenham Hotspur. This time the London club ran out 4–0 winners at the same venue.

Replacing ex-Wolves man Geoff Sidebottom, Withers held his place in the Villa side for almost four years before losing out to new signing John Dunn from Torquay United.

Twice voted as supporters Terrace Trophy Player of the Year in 1966–67, when the team lost his First Division status, and again in 1967–68, Withers amassed a total of 163 senior appearances for Blues' arch-rivals before transferring to Lincoln City for £2,000 in June 1969. He made only one first-class appearance for the Imps and later assisted the Dutch club Go Ahead Deventer and also Atherstone Town (with ex-Blues midfielder Johnny Vincent), eventually announcing his retirement in the summer of 1975.

Colin then became a hotelier in Blackpool and after that was a licensee in Bridgnorth, Shropshire.

Frank Womack

Date of birth: 16 September 1888, Wortley, Attercliffe near Sheffield
Died: 8 October 1968, Caister-on-Sea, Lincolnshire

Blues record:
Appearances: League 491, FA Cup 24, Wartime 92
Goals: 0
Debut: League, 5 September 1908 v Gainsborough Trinity (a) won 3–1

Also played for: Rawmarsh Albion, Worcester City (player-manager)
Managed: Torquay United, Grimsby Town (two spells), Leicester City, Notts County and Oldham Athletic

Blues' greatest-ever full-back and, indeed, the club's finest captain, Frank Womack skippered the side for 17 consecutive seasons during his 20 years at St Andrew's. He made 515 first-class appearances for Birmingham – only goalkeeper Gil Merrick has made more (551). His total of 491 League appearances has stood as a club record since 1928 and his tally of 92 outings was the most made by a Blues player during World War One.

Able to occupy both full-back positions, with no real preference, although he was mainly right footed, Womack was an ever present in 1911–12 and was a regular in Blues' line up, injuries permitting, from 1909 to 1928. Unlucky not to win a full England cap, the nearest he came was to play in three international trials, serve as a reserve twice and represent the Football League on two occasions. He was certainly on a par with Jesse Pennington, but unfortunately he couldn't dislodge the Albion man from the left-back position and during the 1920s there seemed to be several other defenders ahead of him in the pecking order.

Nevertheless, Womack produced some outstanding performances for Blues, gaining a Second Division Championship medal in 1921, this being his only prize as a League player, but he deserved much more. He had a habit of clapping his hands before heading the ball, and perhaps his only weakness was a tendency to lose his position when Blues were on the attack – but thankfully his centre-half was there to cover him. Always wanting to be involved in the action, he would often shout for the ball even if it was 50 yards away!

Womack's 500th senior appearance for Blues ended in a 1–0 defeat at Tottenham in August 1927, while his last outing was against Newcastle United at home in April 1928. He was 39 years and 207 days old at the time – the oldest player ever to appear in a first-class match for the club. The following month he became the first player-manager in the Birmingham League when he was appointed by Worcester City, whom he led to the League title and to the first round of the FA Cup in 1928–29. In July 1930 he became manager of Torquay United but didn't have a happy time at Plainmoor, the Gulls suffering some heavy defeats, among them 10–2 at Fulham and 7–0 at Crystal Palace.

In May 1932 Womack took charge of Grimsby Town and an unbeaten 11-match run at the end of that season took the Mariners to safety. The following season they won the Second Division title and then finished sixth in the top flight, also reaching the semi-finals of the FA Cup in 1936, beaten by Arsenal. In October 1936 he left Blundell Park to take over Leicester City, who were 21st in Division Two. Amazingly, he turned things round at Filbert Street, leading the Foxes to the title. However, after they were relegated in May 1939 he resigned.

In 1940 Womack was suspended for a year after being implicated in a financial irregularities scandal while in charge of Leicester. Frank did not return to football until May 1942 when he became manager of Notts County, where he found Jackie Sewell who became the country's costliest footballer when he joined Sheffield Wednesday for £34,500 in 1951. He left Meadow Lane in 1943 and in February 1945 took over as manager of Oldham Athletic, getting the job ahead of 60 other applicants. Frank resigned in April 1947 and four years later returned as caretaker manager of Grimsby after Charlie Spencer had been taken ill. He left football for good in May 1951.

Womack was involved in a bribery scandal in 1913 when he was offered 55 guineas to 'fix' the result of a League game between his club (Blues) and his future club (Grimsby Town) so that it ended in a draw. He reported the incident to the Blues' secretary who in turn notified the police. A trap was set, and after handing over the money to Womack the culprit was arrested, charged and later found guilty, serving a short sentence in Stafford gaol.

Frank Worthington

Date of birth: 23 November 1948, Halifax, Yorkshire

Blues record:

Appearances: League 71+4, FA Cup 7, League Cup 6
Goals: League 29, FA Cup 2, League Cup 2
Debut: League, 1 December 1979 v Leicester City (h) lost 2–1

Also played for: Huddersfield Town, Leicester City, Bolton Wanderers, Philadelphia Fury (NASL), Tampa Bay Rowdies (NASL), Leeds United, Sunderland, Southampton, Brighton & Hove Albion, Tranmere Rovers (player-manager), Preston North End (player-coach), Stockport County, Cape Town Spurs (player-coach, South Africa), Chorley, Stalybridge Celtic, Galway United (Ireland), Weymouth, Radcliffe Borough, Guiseley, Hinckley Town (player-manager) and England (2 Under-23 and 8 full caps)

Frank Worthington was a good, old-fashioned swashbuckling centre-forward, a soccer nomad, whose career spanned 27 years, during which time he served no fewer than 11 Football League clubs, two in America, one in South Africa and seven at non-League level. He netted close to 300 goals in 905 appearances in major competitions (at home and abroad), his League record being 236 goals in 757 games. He actually scored in each of 22 consecutive League seasons, 1966–67 to 1987–88 inclusive.

Anyone who saw Worthington play will have their own personal thoughts and memories of an immensely skilful footballer. He had the ability to control the ball with one touch, turn and beat a player or shoot at goal with his second. His seemingly casual approach, his occasional arrogant nature and his fiery temper, earned him a 'bad boy' image but there's no doubt he was certainly a class act, a larger than life figure both on and off the field – a real character and a terrific footballer. His ill-concealed disdain of the regimented tactics employed during the 1970s probably cost him several international caps. He received only eight at senior level for England – he deserved far more.

An Elvis Presley fan, Worthington started out with Huddersfield Town as an apprentice in 1964, turned professional in 1966 and moved to Leicester City for £70,000 in 1972, before travelling around the country and abroad, even turning down a move to Liverpool at one point in the mid-1970s. He had his best years at Filbert Street, notching 72 goals in 210 outings, but he also did well at Bolton and Birmingham. Signed by his former manager Ian Greaves for a then club record fee of £90,000 in 1977, he scored 38 goals for Bolton, one of them a real cracker against Ipswich Town at Burnden Park, which was seen and admired by millions on BBC's *Match of the Day* and was voted Goal of the Season.

During his time with Blues, for whom he netted 33 times in 88 games, Worthington became a firm favourite with the fans after helping the team gain promotion from the Second Division in 1980, having earlier done likewise with Huddersfield and Bolton, both of whom went up as champions.

On leaving St Andrew's in March 1982, Worthington joined Leeds United for £100,000 (in a deal involving Welsh international Byron Stevenson) and later cost Sunderland £50,000 (December 1982) and Southampton £30,000 (June 1983). He took over as manager at Tranmere in a blaze of publicity but was not a great motivator, nor was he able to communicate all that well with players. He had very little money to spend in the transfer market, although he did net 21 goals for the Birkenhead side before being sacked with the club at a very low ebb. He gave good service to Brighton, Preston and Stockport to a certain degree, his presence on the pitch proving decisive at times. He was 42 years of age when he played his last competitive game of football for Hinckley Town in 1991. His last appointment in football was as a coach of Halifax Town during the 1991–92 season.

Worthington's eight England appearances came over a period of five months between May and November 1974, the first against Northern Ireland (won 1–0), the last versus Portugal in a European Championship qualifier (0–0). He scored two international goals versus Argentina (2–2) and Bulgaria (won 1–0). In 1991 he was awarded a testimonial by the PFA for his services to football. The game took place at St Andrew's and over 7,000 fans turned up to say 'thank you'. Nowadays he is on the after-dinner speaker's circuit and lives in the village of Shelf near his home town of Halifax. His brothers Dave and Bob, both of whom were full-backs, and his nephew Gary were also professional footballers.

Ron Wylie

Date of birth: 6 August 1933, Kelvin, Glasgow, Scotland

Blues record:
Appearances: League 125+3, FA Cup 13, League Cup 8
Goals: League 2, FA Cup 0, League Cup 0
Debut: League, 21 August 1965 v Crystal Palace (h) won 2–1

Also played for: Clydesdale Juniors, Notts County, Aston Villa, Scotland (2 Schoolboy caps)
Managed: West Bromwich Albion, Coventry City (assistant manager), Cyprus FC (head coach and advisor), Bulova (Hong Kong, head coach)

Barrel-chested Glaswegian Ron Wylie was a cultured footballer, a shrewd and slick inside-forward or wing-half with plenty of skill and determination. A Scottish Schoolboy international (gaining two caps as a 14-year-old), he joined Notts County as an amateur in April 1949, turned professional in September 1950 and made his League debut for the Magpies against Doncaster Rovers in October 1951. He went on to score 39 goals in 238 appearances for the Meadow Lane club, playing alongside Tommy Lawton several times before transferring to Aston Villa for £9,250 in November 1958, signed by the manager who 'found' him initially, Eric Houghton.

Wylie spent seven years at Villa Park, collecting a Second Division Championship medal in 1960 and a League Cup-winners' tankard 12 months later against Rotherham United, while amassing a record of 26 goals in 244 outings for Blues' second city rivals. Having just been voted Midland Footballer of the Year, it was thought that he may well have been past his best when he moved to St Andrew's on a free transfer in July 1965, signed by manager Stan Cullis two months after Blues had been relegated from the top flight. However, he proved everyone wrong by going on to serve the club for five years, adding experience and know-how to the team while accumulating 149 senior appearances and scoring two goals.

Wylie linked up in midfield initially with Malcolm Beard, winger Alec Jackson and Bobby Thomson and later with Trevor Hockey. He did well in his first season, missing only four League games as Blues finished a moderate 10th in Division Two. The following term he was plagued by injury and played in only half of the matches, missing the two-leg League Cup semi-final defeat by Queen's Park Rangers.

Now engaged as team captain, and with Johnny Vincent aiding and abetting him in the engine room, Wylie was back to full fitness and in good form in 1967–68 as Blues just missed out on two prizes, finishing fourth in the League table and losing that Cup semi-final against local rivals and future employers West Bromwich Albion, at his former home, Villa Park. He also netted his two goals for the club during this campaign, both in home League games, the first against Blackpool (lost 2–1), the second versus Plymouth Argyle (drew 2–2). In 1968–69 he was handed 30 outings, but Blues were still finding it hard going in the Second Division, eventually claiming seventh place.

Wylie was not getting any younger and after making just four appearances (three as a substitute) in 1969–70 he announced his retirement with a total of 551 League games under his belt. He was appointed as public relations officer at St Andrew's but held the job for only three weeks before returning to Villa Park as a coach, a position he held until April 1972, following Villa's Third Division Championship success. He later took a coaching position with Coventry City and was assistant manager at Highfield Road from 1978 to 1981 (under Gordon Milne) before coaching Cyprus FC and then Bulova of Hong Kong. In July 1982 he was appointed team manager of West Bromwich Albion, succeeding Ronnie Allen. He didn't have the greatest of times at The Hawthorns and was dismissed in February 1984, quickly returning for another spell as coach at Villa Park, being placed in charge of the club's second team. He remained in office until May 1987 and thereafter acted as a scout for several other League clubs up and down the country before returning to Villa Park for a fourth time in August 1990, as community officer, later accepting the position of community liaison officer (from August 1995).